UNDER THE PARISH LANTERN

John O'Brenner
1976

The author writes:

'This was a land of cider, fat bacon and bread pudding. Of little master men who are gone. Gone too are the snaky bends in the lanes where the hawthorn hedges combed wisps of hay from loaded waggons. The straightened roads, wire fenced, stand stark and naked. Concrete kerbs have replaced roadside verges cut by the roadman's stock-axe, but it is still a good place to live. There is the smell of the new mown hay, the lambs gambol in apple blossomed orchards—and no street lamps, so we are still "Under the Parish Lantern".'

Under the Parish Lantern

Fred Archer

CORONET BOOKS
Hodder Paperbacks Ltd., London

Copyright © 1969 by Fred Archer
First published by Hodder & Stoughton Ltd.
1969
Coronet edition 1973
Second impression 1973
Third impression 1974
Fourth impression 1975

Printed in Great Britain
for Coronet Books, Hodder Paperbacks Ltd.,
St Paul's House, Warwick Lane, London, EC4P 4AH,
by Richard Clay (The Chaucer Press), Ltd.,
Bungay, Suffolk.

ISBN 0 340 17864 7

FOREWORD

'THE FUNNY thing about civilisation is that so many of us take the first opportunity to get the hell out of it,' said a friend of mine the other day, 'at least for long summer breaks and, if we are lucky, for long weekends.' But this wasn't always so. Dr. Johnson said, 'When a man is tired of London he is tired of life.' He rejoiced that 'the full tide of human existence is at Charing Cross', and it took all Boswell's persuasion to get him up to Scotland and the Hebrides. She went on to remind me that John Donne spoke of 'the barbarousness and insipid dullness of the country', how Elizabeth Montagu described her father breaking out 'with a wild exclamation saying that living in the country was like sleeping with one's eyes open', and that when Augustus Hare dined with Lady Combomere, she declared that 'only two people ever had any excuse for living in the country and they were Adam and Eve'.

Her words led me to reflect on the tremendous changes brought about by the motor car and two World Wars and the increasing pressures of town and city life. The more the towns and cities got choked, the more people looked for a chance to escape. And escape they did, in their millions, by road and rail, in trailer caravans and Dormobiles, by bicycle and on foot, until now it is the countryside that is threatened with choking. In the future we are told that human dwellings may cover most of the world's face, and perhaps a good deal of the sea. I read a few weeks ago of a project for building a polythene city over the Indian Ocean, to house sixty or seventy million of the Indian overspill.

We flee to the country for quiet, for sleep, for change of rhythm, for fresh air, for unwinding, for healing. And, as it seems to me, not to escape from civilisation, but to escape back to it at root level. For the village community was always one of man's biggest achievements in living.

Civilisation is based on force, the force that tamed and continues to tame man's environment and bend it to his needs. At last, after a long struggle with the forces of nature, it became possible for men to be civil to each other and to themselves, which is after all exactly what civilisation means. At first all man's time was given to hunting and tilling the soil, to defending himself and his family and to procreating his kind. But after centuries, by clearing forests, by ploughing and sowing, by fencing his fields, by breeding his own cattle, by organising himself into tiny communities, he provided the groundwork for civilising himself. He won for himself sufficient spare time to express himself in painting, in ornament, in writing and playing games, many of which imitate the struggle for life itself.

His reverence for fertility and for the yearly harvest crystallised in religion, in the worship of Demeter, in the yearly maypole dance, in songs such as 'John Barleycorn', in the building of temples, in music and sculpture. But the groundwork was always the soil. Virgil knew that, so did the Greeks. The base of the pyramid was always the husbandman. Civilisation stood on his shoulders.

Thus the farmer and the soil tiller and the community that grew up around them, church and what went on inside it, school, inn, blacksmith, wheelwright, carpenter, the village and its inter-relationships and dependencies is the whole of civilisation in miniature. The church, revamped through the centuries, through early English and decorated and transitional and perpendicular, with maybe an eighteenth-century Sunday school standing beside it; the big house of early Tudor with original tapestries, paintings, furniture and pewter; the village school studying the three Rs and local history and geography and a little French and Latin and a lot of nature study. The man who could plough two acres a day, the man who could make a highly sophisticated machine like a waggon and the man who could fit it with its ironware (then bowl fast in-swingers on Saturday afternoons) the rector, the district nurse, the innkeeper, the schoolmaster, the wise woman, the glee singers, all bound together by ties of blood, business, mutual need or just plain gossip and envy, formed a community which at its best has never been improved upon, one of the peaks of man's achievement. So it isn't to escape from civilisation that people flood out of towns and cities, but to escape back to it, to start learning the civilities all over again.

In the process we have learned to revise our opinion of the countryman and of farm labouring. When I was a small boy fifty years ago, the farm labourer, like the miner, was thought to be little removed from the animal creation. No one knew or cared about the craft and subtlety of general farm work, of the illiterate peasant who could take a dozen or more highly skilled jobs in his stride, ploughing, sowing, reaping and thrashing, who was horseman and cowman and tolerable shepherd, who could hedge, ditch and build a wall, put up a gate and repair a barn. But the tide was already turning against a classical education plus the playing field as the one and only foundation for a true-born Englishman; and thank God for it.

In this revolution the writers have played an honourable part. Gibbs's *Cotswold Village* (1898, I think) was followed by Gertrude Jekyll's account of cottage life in Surrey, Sturt's *Wheelwright's Shop, Memoirs of a Surrey Labourer, The Bettesworth Book* and *A Small Boy in the Sixties*, the angry outpourings of J. H. Massingham, the writings of Tom Hennell, John Moore, Henry Warren, Adrian Bell and more recently the superb George Ewart-Evans. I name only a few of a long line. All these along with many others, not forgetting the indispensable *Countryman*, have helped to redress the balance.

And Fred Archer is an honourable member of that illustrious company. In some ways I like him best of all, because he doesn't pretend to be 'a writer' but just a farmer, putting things down in the plainest and most unadorned English, digging into his memory and hauling up great spadesful of practical matter about the village people of his youth (and as we say in Yorkshire, 'There's nowt so queer as folk') about tools, trees, horses, cows and pigs, about the village and its festivals, haymaking, bell-ringing, bee-keeping, tea-fights and magic lantern shows, about hedgers and ditchers, water diviners and village carpenters. And because it is all so patently true, it glows with the magical warmth of the age it re-creates, the England of the First World War and just after, which has now vanished. The days of home farming, horse ploughing and handmilking.

So if you are thinking of taking a trip, leave your LSD and pot behind and come with Fred Archer into lovely Worcestershire. I guarantee you'll enjoy it.

BERNARD MILES

AUTHOR'S PREFACE

ONE OF the many letters I have had since writing *The Distant Scene* reads, 'You have rescued so much that is precious from oblivion. I can hear the characters as if it were yesterday.' This, my second book, reveals I hope more of the secrets of country folk; how they spent their lives as a tale that is told. It is set in that boomerang-shaped land under Bredon Hill between Pigeon Lane, Overbury and Comberton Quay on Shakespeare's Avon, with Ashton-under-Hill in the centre, during the early part of the century.

What is so unique about the people and the land where the morning sun peeps first over the Cotswolds, where the clay bakes hard in the summer sun and still clings lovingly to the boots in winter? There is something uncannily static about the men who worked the land as Queen Victoria's reign ended. Men who used the same tools as their grandfathers; I remember them in their prime, straw hatted, loading and unloading waggons of hay, their horses sweating under the jingling harness and the haymakers under their broad braces, brass-buckled leather belts and leather yorks strapped below the knee. I have seen them wet through digging out winter flushed ditches and then homeward bound in frozen corduroys.

This was a land of cider, fat bacon and bread pudding. Of little master men who are gone. Gone too are the snaky bends in the lanes where the hawthorn hedges combed wisps of hay from loaded waggons. The straightened roads, wire fenced, stand stark and naked. Concrete kerbs have replaced roadside verges cut by the roadman's stock-axe, but it is still a good place to live. There is the smell of the new-mown hay, the lambs gambol in apple-blossomed orchards—and no street lamps, so we are still 'Under the Parish Lantern'.

LIST OF ILLUSTRATIONS

Between pages 80 and 81

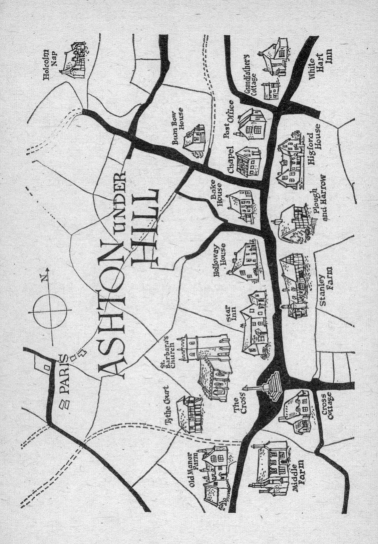

CHAPTER ONE

HOLCOMB NAP

WHEN I think of freedom, my mind goes back to the Nap, or Knolp as the old folk called it. This part of Bredon has such a varied history; for generations, stone for the roads was quarried from the flat but the southerly slope was a playground for children. On this slope grew a wiry type of grass—very slippery to climb when the sun had baked the underlying clay to a hard pan in the height of summer. Rough sledges were made by us boys out of old cider barrels and during the holidays we careered at terrific speed down the slope from the quarry on the top, then past the two coppices—the primrose coppice and violet coppice—until we reached a row of withies at the foot and by careful manoeuvring landed safely on the bridle road.

Holcomb Nap is one of those names, Anglo-Saxon in origin, which means exactly what it says—Hollycomb, the combe where the holly grows. Holly at one time was used for religious ceremonies but as my friend Job Barley told me, 'Holly, my bwoy, a bin used for the swingel or short stick on the end of the flail long afore the remembrance of mon, and besides,' he said, 'what does old Walt use for his whip sticks? Why, holly of course.'

Before our squire took over the Nap it had belonged to a family of squires for three to four hundred years. The gorse bloomed there all the year round and a row of old elder, or ellum, trees followed the streamlet running from the little pool at the top. A heady scent is the blow of the elder and the wine from the berries acted as a harmless sleeping draught on some of our villagers. The stunted hawthorns, a show of white in May and a harbour for the hungry fieldfare in winter, provided a meagre harvest of mistletoe for Christmas. I wonder, did the Druids cut this mistletoe with their golden sickles long ago?

This little bit of England seems steeped in the history of sport and religion. The badgers' earths are still there and the vixens still give birth to their cubs in the primrose coppice and move to the big Ashton Wood where there is so much cover. The squire,

that auburn-haired, wax-moustached bachelor, was lord of all
he surveyed and hunted twice a week, Jim Jinks, his groom,
getting his jet black horse ready for the meets around the hill.
Holcomb Nap lies in a direct line from Big Wood to Grafton
Firs, and so often the field had that stretch of sideland ground
to cover as the fox made for the firs.

CHAPTER TWO

THE BARN, THE BROOK AND THE BRIDGE

HAVE YOU ever entered a cathedral, the sun glistening through the stained-glass windows, the smell of old timber, the weathered stone floor? What an atmosphere this all creates. There is a feeling that for hundreds of years people have met here in times of trouble and joy.

Now enter our old Cross Barn, thatched roof moss covered, timber built with square panels filled with wattle and daub, two doors on massive hinges fastened by a hinge asp and staple beat out on the anvil by the local blacksmith long since laid to rest. These doors are in the middle with another two off-side; each set, when thrown wide open, are big enough for the largest of waggons to pass through. The floor is made of blue lias flag stones, level and clean. This is commonly known as the Sheep Barn, the shepherd having pride of place for its use. On the right of the door the sheep-pens have stood, with the little door to the fold that seems to me so biblical. The partition walls are of sawn elm—sawn long ago in the old squire's saw pit. The elm boards, being vertical, are nailed to long larch poles grown near the parish quarry almost on the summit of our hill. If a board becomes displaced, it is easy to see that the nails are also locally made—probably by the Evesham nailers in Nailers' Row, that row of houses in Bengeworth where these men had each his little forge in the garden. Thinking of these industrious people, it is easy to realise how many of our local houses and buildings are braced together with these little works of art in metal.

Thomas Hardy describes the threshing floor and the sheep shearing in these old barns. The Cross Barn had its threshing floor and the sound of the flail threshing the corn had been heard there within living memory. My friend Walt told me that he first used the flail in that barn. 'We was a-threshing beans, me and old Josey Summers. Now when you stands opposite and works together you brings your hinged stick down in turn. Well, ya see,' he says, 'I got sort of out of step with old Josey and ketched him the master smack with my flail on top of his yud. My boy, didn't he tell me my fortune!' Josey was laid to rest years after under the churchyard wall. Walt died this year aged 87; the flails are just museum pieces.

When Shepherd Marsh was lambing his ewes in the barn, he made little private wards for the mothers, divided by thatched hurdles. A hurricane lamp swung from a broken plough trace was all the light he had. Here were his headquarters where he fussed the weakly lambs, drenched the ailing ewe and later in the year did his shearing on a large hessian sheet spread over the threshing floor. His hand shears clipped away all day and shone like silver as they went through the egg-yolk-coloured wool near the sheep. His fleeces were rolled so tightly they could have been kicked all around the barn without mishap. These were stacked on a staging made of hurdles so that the air could circulate and prevent mould.

The barn with its old timbers all numbered at the joints had had a varied history. In the autumn the shepherd didn't need the barn; all the sheep were out in the fields with the rams. Then the sights and smells changed as the apple pickers brought in loads of keeping apples and tipped them on a bed of straw, leaving them until the market was right. The men had a wet-day job picking them up, grading them and packing them in sixty-pound hampers.

What of the repairs to the barn? Oliver, an absolute gem with his tools, cut down whole ash trees and replaced some of the uprights—if they were crooked, he found a crooked one. Any small roof repairs he did with cleft withy poles and Ernest the Thatcher patched the holes the sparrows had made with wheat straws pegged down with withies.

The shepherd was fond of his barn and couldn't abide the Dutch barn. 'Thur bin never any good hay come out o' them contraptions,' he said.

Our village, being at the foot of the hill, or where the hill and vale met, has an abundant supply of water oozing out of the slopes. One such stream is Holcomb Brook, flowing from the Big Wood, past the badger earths, the coppice where the aconite and bluebell make their carpets in the spring, and down in the vale. At right angles to Holcomb Brook, as it passes through my field 'Big Holbrook', there runs a ditch under a row of stunted elms. Nothing unusual about this except that the ditch runs two ways. The land, falling to north and to south, makes the water which goes north follow the parish boundary to Hinton and empty into the Avon at Evesham. The part of the ditch which runs south joins Holcomb Brook which runs into Carrant Brook, winding its sluggish, weary way to join the Avon at Tewkesbury. The two streams join the river twenty miles apart.

Carrant Brook is the one closely connected with our village. A watering place for cattle, with withy trees, both common and red, lining its banks, watercress growing at the sides and a few eels living in the deeper parts. In winter it floods the meadows and the rabbits forsake their holts in its banks and climb the hollow withy trees. These trees provide little cities of refuge for them as they lie high and dry in the roxy peaty tops often covered with ivy and bramble. The wood-pigeons feed on the ivy berries in winter. One or two fords exist where the cattle cross, but mostly the banks are steep with a mass of kingcups, ragged robin and meadowsweet, with its heady, rather sickly smell in high summer. The shade provides protection from the sun for the cows and the streams are alive with flies and insects of all kinds, including the occasional dragonfly with its wings of gold.

The brook has several bridges in the parish, the one in the Back Lane, or Gipsies' Lane, being quite old and made of local stone. Hard by this bridge, a matter of fifteen yards away, there are the stone remains either side of the brook of a much earlier bridge. This coincided with an ancient track known as 'Deviaton Saltway' which was used in Roman times.

Bridges fascinate me. When the brook is almost at flood level, it foams as it rushes past the pebbles, the fallen withies and the rest of the flotsam and jetsam which accumulates on awkward bends producing little waterfalls.

One bridge very dear to me I haven't mentioned yet. At the bottom of the First Ham, an L-shaped meadow, a large withy tree, ripe with age and split down the centre, lies on the edge of the brook. Half the tree, shaped like a half moon, falls across the Carrant Brook and has taken root on the other bank, making an ideal natural bridge. We crossed and recrossed that bridge hundreds of times. In winter it was frightening as the waters rushed below, but oh in the summer it was the place to sit and catch an eel or two, or just a shady spot to watch life as it went on around. When the brook was cleaned to improve the drainage of the hams, or water meadows, my little bridge had to go. You see it was slowing the progress of the water downstream to the Avon and so on to the River Severn and the sea.

There is really nothing that mere man can make that is quite so quaint, so beautiful as a withy bridge, covered with moss and a part of the very earth itself. With the cleaning of our brook the watercress went too, and the wild mint, with its almost intoxicating smell; brook lime, a persistent plant, remained on the bank which was riddled with the holes of water voles.

It strikes me that the brook was so much like life itself. First the slow, lazy rippling stream, as life is taken for granted in our youth, then, like the brook after it has cleared itself of its hindrances—the seemingly unimportant things—it seems to fly past. Christmas days are here before we are ready, just another milestone—and we are not even promised seventy of these. How ageless are the hills, the trees, the church, the roads and paths compared with the little time we are allowed to enjoy these things. Looking through my window I see a winter's scene in the orchard. The trees are bare, the only green being the mistletoe and the ivy growing up the crooked trunks of the old, gnarled cider apple trees. Starlings are greedily clearing up the remains of the cull apples carpeting the grass, the stream through the orchard has not so far to travel before it reaches the brook; it is really just the overflow from the moat where as a lad I caught the occasional roach and set night lines for eels. Our moat is no ordinary moat. It lies in a hollow at the back of the church where, in the close, the outline of the moated house, long since gone, is easily traced. The moat is really the monks' fishpond. This would have been most useful. Living about eighty miles from the sea, they would never taste sea fish and depended on the freshwater fish. The source is easily traced, the spring water boiling up out of the hill between two old oaks which again seem ageless.

CHAPTER THREE

THE OLD SQUIRE

STINT WORKED at the Manor, living in one of the Squire's cottages opposite. 'Stint,' said the old Squire one day, 'thee bist a good workman and I be going to give thee a rise in wages.' 'Thank ya, gaffer, that ull help a lot. Very good on ye, I be sure.' Some weeks after, the Squire said, 'Stint, I allus have been a man of my word. I'm giving you an extra shilling a week, but your cottage is worth a bit more rent, so if I charge another shilling for that, that ull square it.'

The Squire did not always get the best of it in our village. Widow Taplin kept the tollgate at the end of the Groaten; the charge was twopence and the Squire had the knack of by-passing the turnpike by crossing the Naits on his journeys to Evesham. But one day he went by the Groaten, and Widow Taplin drew the gate across and asked for her due. The Squire threw a golden sovereign down in the mud saying, 'Pick that up and give me the change.' Not to be outdone, the Widow brought nineteen shillings and tenpence in copper and threw the lot in front of the Squire's horse. 'Now thee pick that lot up.' Besides keeping the Tollgate, Widow Taplin sold sweets and was, according to Lofty the Ladder-maker, very religious. As her second husband, she married the blind postman, who delivered letters with the aid of his dog, Shackles.

Though the old Squire watched his pennies, he could be generous. When the first train ran on our branch line, he gave a great feast for the villagers, with a hogshead of cider. There were sports and donkey races when the train had passed through; boys stood on the railway to watch it coming.

The Manor was said to be haunted by a ghost which repeatedly walked the stairs and made footprints in the snow just outside the back door, going a few steps and then back to the cellar. The Squire called in the parson to lay the ghost, and the ceremony of exorcism was completed by bricking in a barrel of wine in the cellar to pacify the evil spirit. As Fred Wheatcroft said to me, 'Thur be things as appears as we beunt meant to understand. They be only understood by the One above, like the Friar's dream at Beckford.' The Friar of Beckford, so the story went, had a dream that a pot of gold lay buried by the gate leading into a field known as The Gaskins. He got up early and found it just where he dreamed it would be. After his death in a little cottage near the church of St. John, gold coins were found under the floor. Besides the Manor ghost, there was a White Lady said to walk up and down Gipsies' Lane on moonlight nights, sometimes changing herself into a cat.

The Squire was now getting old and more childish. One day he told Lofty and Charlie Bradfield to come into the dining room. 'We be going to have some sport,' he said. A galvanised bath was placed on the table, the Squire half filled it with port wine and then out into the barn next the bull-pen he went and fetched in a brood of young ducks. Placing these in the bath he said, 'Now thee watch,' and they swam around in the port wine. It became obvious that the Squire would not last much longer and, being a bachelor, his young nephew Humphrey would be following him.

CHAPTER FOUR

THE YOUNG SQUIRE

HUMPHREY, NEPHEW of the man who had held the reins in our village life for so long, was tall, lithe and handsome in the extreme. He had served in one of the Guards regiments. Taking over the estate of 800 acres at the age of twenty-four was quite a venture for him.

Meets of the hounds at the Manor were great occasions. Humphrey, immaculate in his hunting pink and silk hat, rode a thoroughbred bay mare, and it goes without saying, human nature being what it is, that he had a following of eligible young lady admirers. He became very friendly with a young bachelor from the next village. They were both hard riders and were usually there at the kill. Humphrey's friend, Roland, used to say, 'If you can't start a fox in Ashton Wood, it's no good drawing Beckford Coppice.' It has been said that Roland never saw a fox on our hill and more often than not his horse could be seen tied up to a beech tree with some attractive young lady's horse tied by the side. Roland liked horses but he also liked women, and when the note on the hunting horn sounded 'gone to ground', Roland and his latest fancy could be described as doing the same.

Oliver, the rabbit catcher and rough carpenter, clearing his throat with a well-aimed spit after chewing his twist tobacco, said, 'Why, there ha bin more bones made up in these coppices on hunting day than ever have bin broke. Humphrey and Roland,' added Oliver, 'live like two fighting cocks and if they had to work like me, them lady things unn't worry um.'

As the stream of life flowed on, slow and content as the Carrant Brook, Humphrey and Roland wined, dined and hunted and had everything that money could buy.

Frank Wheatcroft, a boy-chap as Oliver called him, worked for the owner of a neighbouring brickyard. His job was to take the lady of the house out in the polished brown governess cart with navy blue padded seats and brass-handled lamps. This was drawn by Polly, a liver chestnut mare clad in silver mounted brown harness. Jim Morris, who owned the brickworks, had three beautiful daughters—Ruth, Esther and Sarah. 'Mind tha,' Frank would say, 'you ud think that butter udn't melt in their mouths but a good lump a cheese udn't choke um. They'm warm, mind.'

Frank drove the buggy on some Saturday nights to Winchcombe, taking the three sisters to a dance there. Young Squire Humphrey and Roland drove over in the Squire's trap which was pulled by a lively cob, not content to trot but at a canter three ha'pence for tuppence, and after a livener at the Hobnails, they were ready for all kinds of developments. Frank, who was in charge of the Morris girls, shut his horse out, stabled it and had to wait late into these nights to bring them home to Ashton. He developed a friendship with Police-Sergeant McQuire, an Irishman and an old-time copper, so necessary at dances even in those days.

In the summer, Flannel Dances were held on the hotel lawn. The women were dressed in tennis dresses and the men in cream flannel trousers. Falling steeply from this level, springy turf was a rose garden with walks and a summer-house, and with the air heavy with the smell of night-scented stocks, Frank said, 'They ud start their sweethearting.'

Sergeant McQuire, drawing Frank from the bar parlour of the hotel, took him to the edge of the rose garden: 'Sure, faith and begorrah, Frank, do you know how the gentry of your country live?' Frank beheld the various stages of love and romance as Humphrey and Roland wooed Ruth and Esther Morris— Sarah having found a partner, the son of the manager of her father's brickworks.

During the early hours of Sunday morning Frank started for home, a tired boy, driving a governess cart with three amorous girls who had really had too much champagne to be good for them. Hell for leather behind came Humphrey and Roland in their trap approaching the Sister Elms—two elm trees, one on either side of the road, the road narrowing at this point so that there was only room for one vehicle. Humphrey and Roland passed the buggy and drew their cob up on to the wide grass verge. Humphrey asked Ruth if she would ride home in his trap and Roland accompanied Frank and the other Morris girls in the governess cart. Ruth, with that twinkle in her carefree eye and swept right off her feet by the young squire, consented. Roland took the reins from Frank, drove on a few yards and then drew the horse to a halt. The night was keen and starry, the moon at the full, and Humphrey embraced Ruth against one of the Sister Elms. Ruth, remembering her Sunday School days, said, 'You know there is One above who can see all.' The rest of the party listened with interest as an old owl, perched on the top of the elm, answered Tu whit, tu woo.

While Humphrey and Roland lived life 'topped up and brimming over', Roland cared little about his farm, which was left in the capable hands of Bert Lively, an all-rounder, as he would have been described on the cricket field, and carter Bill Stokes. Peaceful England, when life had not become cheap and meaningless and when a frail of meat could be had for a shilling on these pre-refrigerator Saturday nights when the shopping by gaslight continued until near midnight.

The old Manor Farm had a fine set of nag stables, divided into stalls, glazed tiles of cream on the wall, iron mangers, water troughs and hay racks. In fact those stables were away ahead of their time. Next to the harness room, with the iron frames to hang up the saddles and bridles, was a small room for the groom, complete with fireplace—a bedsitter in fact. Adjoining this was a trap house to accommodate traps, gigs and governess carts.

Up a wide staircase above the stables in the gabled, ornamental-tiled Victorian building was a well-floored airy room known as the Ballroom. To call it a ballroom was perhaps rather presumptuous, but the fact was that dances were held there on some Saturday nights, the remaining members of the church orchestra providing the music. In the old Squire's time, the place was used as a granary for his corn, but Humphrey and Roland had to have somewhere to entertain their friends in splendour and gaiety.

Humphrey became friendly with a London stockbroker—a widower who had a beautiful auburn-haired daughter named Mildred. Frank Wheatcroft called her 'a Cockney tart with enough Robin starch on her face to starch my shirt, plastered with rouge and her's forty if her's a day—not a bad pair o' shafts, mind'.

On these dance nights in the ballroom, Jasper Hill and Frank Wheatcroft took care of the horses, stabling them in the roomy nag stable, and parking the traps and governess carts in the trap house as the horses, sweaty and tired, arrived bringing their little loads of lovers. How well they were cared for, fed and watered. When the harness had been hung on the walls of the harness room, Jasper and Frank retired to the groom's room and sat around the fire drinking their accustomed rough cider. Humphrey sent one of the maids down with a plate of ham sandwiches—these Saturday nights were nights to remember.

'What dost thou think of that London tart, Jasper?' said Frank, who was a little younger, a little more gallus, than Jasper.

'Her unt having a very good influence on our young gaffer,' said Jasper. 'Her's out to trap him, thee'll see.'

Taking another sip of some of the Squire's best cider, Frank spoke his mind. 'I'll tell thee what though, I'd sooner be spending the evening along with her than along with thee.'

'Now thee bist a-talking summat stupid, Frank. What good dust thee think thee udst be to her, thee couldn't keep up with her ways. This cider and the cheese we buys Saturday from A'sum [Evesham] udn't do for her, mind. You remembers how we has to break the cheese with a ploughshare it's that devilish hard. Oh no, it's no good a-thinking o' courting one o' them butterflies without you got the coppers. Champagne and salmon out o' the Severn, her's having, I a bin told by the butcher.'

When the music died down and the young, the carefree and careless were finally ready for home, Jasper and Frank led the various collection of horses, nags, cobs and ponies and harnessed them in their vehicles, each collecting quite a little windfall in the way of tips before the little crowd of merrymakers went their separate ways.

Mildred had learned to ride at a London riding school. Frank and Jasper, unaccustomed to seeing such a modern huzzy in our sleepy nook under the hill, criticised her mode of life with unbridled tongues. Of course there was a touch of jealousy in their words. 'A brazen huzzy,' Jasper called her when he saw her riding astride to hounds. 'All the decent lady things ride side saddle with long riding habits. Her and her jodhpurs or whatever they call 'em.'

Jasper spat as he finished another bit of twist tobacco he had been chewing for some time and then talked seriously now about life and the little they knew about love, Jasper divulging a few secrets he knew about women and about his wife Hannah when she was in the family way. 'Her only went out nights, different to what they be in London, mind, they be forruder there.' Jasper told how he took Hannah on one of her exercises down the Blacksmiths' Lane arm in arm. 'Her was about seven months gone,' he confided to Frank. 'Thee ut understand one day when the missus refuses the morning cup of tea.' At that time Joe Baker was carter for young Freddy Burman and a mare he called Violet was down with gripes after eating too many apples in the Tythe Court Orchard. Now the important thing with gripes, after the usual dose of half linseed oil and half turpentine, is to keep the horse walking to get the wind moving again. Jasper was exercising Hannah on this bright moonlight October night, the stars twinkling and the owls hooting, and just a touch of hoar frost or 'bit of rime' on the grassy bank of the village street. It was an odd sight and one of the young Bradfields watched the scene—Hannah on Jasper's arm, Violet with Joe. Young Bradfield ran in the house, startling the others as he announced, 'I do believe Jasper's missus a got the gripes.'

CHAPTER FIVE

NEDDY WHISTLER

NEDDY GOT his name Whistler after he left our little village and became a lamp-lighter and douter in Evesham. Neddy was nervous douting the gas lamps near the old churchyard, so he whistled. He saw a white donkey one night and declared it to be a ghost. Quite often after that the lamp near the churchyard burnt merrily on all through the night, Neddy not daring to go near the churchyard again. His father told him, 'If the living don't hurt ya, it's certain the dead won't.'

As an old hand at the gasworks, he had become almost a legend, his ways and his outlook on life were so much out of the ordinary. I remember that when I was a boy he still visited our village with the local papers and the smell of his Woodbine still lingers in my mind when on Friday nights Dad opened the kitchen window to take the paper, Mother shouting from the tea table 'Do mind the lamp' as the paraffin hanging lamp flared up with the extra draught from the open window.

'How much do I owe you, Ned?' Dad would say—he had probably missed paying for the tuppenny paper for a couple of weeks.

'Just a shilling tonight, sir,' Ned replied, another puff of Woodbine clouding over our Friday tea table.

Ned had a very tempestuous passage through life. My old friend Tom Wheatcroft told me: 'I remembers the time when he came round the village selling watercress and mackerel. Hasn't thee ever heard of Ned's watercress ladder? Four rungs and he stood on the middle un.' I hadn't but I did know of some of his exploits at the gasworks—some of his unconscious humour. 'The missus had a baby last night,' he told my uncle one Monday morning. 'Guess what it was.'

'A boy,' was my uncle's guess.

'No,' says Ned, 'guess agun.'

'A girl,' my uncle said.

Ned's reply will never be forgotten in the Vale; these were his very words, 'Why, I be too late, somebody or other must have told ya.'

One Saturday night Ned bought a pair of boots at the foot of Bridge Street, a quarter of a mile from where he lived near the Town Hall of Evesham. As he came in very late his wife asked the classic Evesham question, 'Whur the ell ast bin?' 'Oi a bin to Berkleys and bought a pair of boots and ant I had a game a getting up Bridge Street!' 'Why didn't you cut the string that joins them at the back?' his wife said. 'Never thought,' he replied. Later he told my uncle that he had to 'wear em a month afore he could get them on.'

In our village he worked for a small farmer who kept pigs and poultry.

'Have you watered the pigs?' the farmer said one day.

'No, I forgot,' he muttered as the long ash from his cigarette drooped from his expressionless mouth.

'Straight away water them then,' said the farmer and away went Ned with the three-gallon bucket. Coming back to the house he told the farmer he had watered them 'and my God didn't the little devils holla.'

He had poured it on their backs!

'It's beef I like,' he says, 'and they tells me it's fourpence a pound in America, but lors what a way to fetch it.'

'How long has your father been dead?' my uncle asked him one day.

'Well now, that's a bit of a poser,' said Ned, 'but if he ad a lived until a wick next Tuesday he'd a bin dead just three years last Friday.'

'No wonder our kids a got bad feet,' he told his wife one day, 'thee bist allus a hitting um on the yud with the scrubbing brush.'

Some of his workmates, pulling his leg as usual, told him to apply for the job of hangman at Worcester Jail. 'There's money in it, Ned,' they told him. 'Five pounds a time and the rope thee canst allus sell for a souvenir.' He didn't get the job but another nickname stuck to him for years—that of 'Hangman.'

No, they don't make people like Ned today. He caused more fun, more innocent mirth in his life than ever he knew.

CHAPTER SIX

PARISH MEETINGS

IN THE 1890s a law was passed entitling all villages with a population of over 300 to elect a Parish Council and those smaller to hold Parish Meetings. Up until that time much of the business of running the village affairs was decided at Vestry Meetings. Ashton had over 300 inhabitants and soon availed herself of the privilege of a Parish Council, holding also an annual Parish Meeting, or if necessary an Extraordinary Parish Meeting.

I was always interested in the Parish Meetings. Dad belonged to the Parish Council and I attended the Annual Parish Meeting at an early age. Not being a ratepayer and not having a vote, I just sat and listened to the wisdom of the ancients.

Water oozes out of Bredon Hill at the hamlet of Paris and that's where our reservoir was built in the 1870s. I suppose we folk have always been careful to the extreme when it comes to spending public money. The chief reason was that in the 1870s there were few ratepayers and the load had to be spread on their shoulders alone. Ways were discussed by the, then, Vestry Meeting for piping the water to the village and it was decided to use secondhand gas pipes, which were known in the trade as 'bastard' size, as these were cheap, but they proved to be a great problem when we had bursts as fittings could not be got for them.

In the 1920s when Council houses were built at the top of the village, the pressure of water from Paris just about supplied the stand pipes in the road. By then the R.D.C. prohibited any more tapping of the main for private use. This caused quite a stir. An Extraordinary Parish Meeting was called to be held at the school. A local artist, Chairman of the Parish Council, was chosen as Chairman of the Meeting; a cool, kindly man who went to school with F. E. Smith—later Lord Birkenhead. A surveyor from the R.D.C. attended to give his opinion and explained that there was insufficient pressure to allow the main to be tapped further. Up jumped Henry, a platelayer on the railway line, 'Henry Fly-by-Night' he was known as, and he had come down here from the Black Country with a relaying gang and stayed. 'Yaw knows nought abawt it, your Asum lot; the school governess lives at the 'ighest point in Ashton and thur's plenty of water in her bedroom. I knows 'cos I bin thur.'

'Oh Henry,' said Widow Tomkins our schoolteacher, 'what will people think?'

'That depends on ow foul thur minds ba, don't it? Yaw knows as Oi only done a bit of wallpappering there and that's the gospel!'

'All right, Henry,' the Chairman said when the chuckles had died down a bit. 'But that's interesting that there's sufficient pressure to reach Mrs. Tomkins' bedroom, very interesting indeed.'

Sam from Asum was all the time pondering in his mind how much the previous speakers knew of the situation. Sam was a very observant man; he sank his well where a patch of clover was green all the summer. Water, he said, was rising out of the little school desks we were all cramped in. Sam was bearded, rosy cheeked and dressed in his best jacket and corduroy trousers. He towered above most of us, being six foot three when he was an upright soldier in the Boer War. 'Thur's plenty of water at Paris, it just wants harnessing,' he said. 'If we could only harness it, get a ram and push it up into the plain by the Cuckoo Pen on Little Hill and build a reservoir, we'd 'ave enough pressure to supply all the houses in Ashton.'

Little Mr. Penny, a gentleman gardener, then made some suggestions about a spring running to waste on the Leasow further up the hill which would supply us by gravitation.

'Thee sit down, Master Penny,' said Sam. 'Thee hasn't bin yur long enough in the village to get thee seat warm. Thy logic ain't worth a hatful of crabs.'

Our artist Chairman, George Willoughby said, 'Come, come, Sam, Mr. Penny's suggestion may be worth a thought.'

Tom Wheatcroft, sitting sideways in the desk by me, cupped his mouth with his left hand and whispered, 'Frederick, thee ut understand one day. Sam and Penny aren't first cousins. Master Penny bought a model T Ford yesterday, and Sam called him a hungry-gutted toad and that he ud yut and yut till he bursts.'

The R.D.C. stated that the water up on the Leasow was variable in summer and if we had a dry summer it would be insufficient. Joe Baker, water diviner, disputed this and told us how many thousands of gallons ran to waste through the sheep-wash pool. This, he said, went underground for some distance and boiled up again by Shaw Green. Bill Bosworth, rate collector, doubted if this was the same water but Old Joe was a step ahead. 'I can prove it,' he said. 'I took some permanganate of potash and put a good doing in the Leasow spring and ran down to Shaw Green; the water was running out into that stream the colour of port wine.'

The whole scheme was postponed because in those days all the expense would have fallen on the village and rents plus rates of the Council houses would have had to have been increased by a shilling a week, and the agricultural wage was only 29/3. 'Bucket lavatories—I don't mind emptying them,' Sam said. 'I'll empty anybody's for a consideration.'

'Any other business?' George Willoughby asked. 'Yes, thur is,' Joe Baker said. 'What about all them Gubbing Holes as empties into the ditch at the back of my house?' (Some of the larger houses had invested in septic tanks.) 'The stink from this lot you could cut with a knife in a dry time when the stream off Holcomb Nap runs low. Course I ant rubbed my back against any College wall so you won't take much notice a me, if I had a job and a fine car, that might help.' Mr. Willoughby had a certain sympathy for Joe and instructed the Clerk to contact the Sanitary Inspector to see what could be done. 'We take just as much notice of you, Joe. Even if your education was brief, you have a fund of experience which we all value.' 'Half a minute,' said Sam. 'Thee bist a talking of the ditch in Gipsies' Lane, I udn't like nobody to stop the sewage going down there, I gets my best tomato plants out of that ditch. The gentry be eating more tomatoes now and the seeds starts well in the black silt on the side of that ditch. Master Archer's cows drinks it lower down and it don't seems to hurt 'em.' Dad spoke up then: 'It's all right, we're calf rearing—haven't sent milk away for years.'

'There, gentlemen, thank you all for your interest.' Mr. Willoughby, a master of diplomacy, closed the meeting.

These meetings were places where people could air their views and things which came forward for discussion had most likely been bottled up for months previously. I remember Bill Bosworth's list of complaints: 'That thur hedge in the Chapel Orchard is right over the footpath up Holcomb Lane and scratts Master Whitfield's bus every time he goes up there. It a bin brought up now for three years at least, can't anything be done about it? Then thurs the Station Bridge—as slick as a glass bottle. All right for you gentlemen with cars but a devilishly ackud for me and my pony and trap. Get the clerk to write to the Company.' (The railway was always 'The Company'.)

I think that one must admit the average old-time countryman spoke his mind—not meaning to offend but without wrapping things up. He could give and take and no one bore malice after these meetings. It was quite common for one to say to another next day in the street, 'What I said last night was not to offend, although I knows you thinks different.' 'That's all right,' would come the reply, 'We beun't a goin to fall out over things like that.' One thing I learnt at these gatherings was that if something was said that 'reached you', as the saying is, it was unwise to lose your temper; much better to treat it lightly.

CHAPTER SEVEN

FOOTBALL AND FOOT AND MOUTH

As FAR as I can gather, football was played in our village in the 1890s but it was not until the 1920s that our team, The Tigers, became famous for miles around. Earlier teams had played in the New Piece but the team in the '20s played in the Wynch, that level piece of turf which was just over the stile from our yard and belonged to Mr. Percy Attwood, happily still living and still taking a lively interest in cricket. You see he was at Malvern College with the Fosters. Football in the Wynch brought most of the village out on Saturday afternoons. The Sedgeberrow supporters walked across the fields. As a small boy, I rarely missed a home game. My Aunt Annie knitted me a black and gold woollen mascot shaped like a tiger which I wore on the lapel of my mac.

I remember Happy Annie from Sedgeberrow, but most of all Stodge, the roadman, who used to arrive early and hook the nets on the goal-posts. He was a stocky, lame man who had led a varied life from poaching to driving steam-ploughing tackle. He carried a large jar of cider which, when he waddled, looked half as big as himself. He also brought with him a cider horn to tot out. The players who drank cider had some before the game started and more at half-time when Stodge half ran and half walked onto the field.

If a player got injured, two people rushed onto the field—the trainer Charlie Cuthbert, a ganger on the railway, and Stodge. Charlie attended the injured player, first with the magic sponge, smelling salts and liniment, home-made from eggs and turpentine. As he recovered, Stodge would pour the player out one little horn of cider. If a knee was dislocated, Joe Baker was called—just one more little capability of Joe's.

In their hey-day, our village teams won the First Division, Cheltenham League, three years running, the Cheltenham Hospital Cup, etc.

We all had our idols; mine was Tosh Ballard on the left wing.

Another favourite of mine was George Pearce, a right back. He lofted the ball up to the forwards almost in the goal mouth of our opponents, but when we were winning, say about three to one with ten minutes to play, he often skied the ball into Bowles' walnut tree and the visiting supporters shouted, 'Keep him on the island.' Amusing incidents on the Wynch there were plenty. Titch Pope was so drunk in one match he stayed offside and the Ref ignored him—a pity, we needed his skill and ball control. Our opponents were Bretforton's Old Boys, a strong team.

As a boy I never enjoyed friendly matches—'It's only a Friendly today, it won't be much of a game.' In a Friendly, there wasn't the full-blooded tackle or the charging of the goal-keeper (in order then). But one Friendly was a real scream. Our Goalie didn't turn up so Peggy Boon, a man with a wooden leg, offered to keep goal for our team. His leg was pointed, a real peg shape, and as he manoeuvred from one goal-post to the other watching the ball carefully, he was in a way doing a sort of waltz, one, two, three, one, two, three. He picked the shots of the opposing centre-forward cleanly up in his hands and tipped one or two over the bar until one low, powerful shot made him dive to his right to smother the ball. He lay on the ball with his wooden leg lashing out in all directions and the forwards were wise to let him get on his feet and throw the ball to George Pearce for him to clear upfield. I forget the result of that game but wouldn't have missed seeing Peggy Boon in a goal for any-thing. Said old Stodge, 'If that 'ooden leg had a hit anybody on the yud it ud a knocked their brains out.'

On November 9th, 1924, we were at home to Fairford Town in the North Gloucestershire Senior Cup. There were nearly one thousand spectators on the Wynch. Captain Barton, ex-Indian Army, was in goal and the atmosphere was electric when, with ten minutes to go in this important semi-final, the teams were drawing, one goal each. Suddenly, from a clearance by George Pearce to centre-half Billy Stevens, Billy took a thirty-yard shot at goal with terrific power. The Fairford goalie just couldn't stop this one—waist high, nearly in the corner of the net. Into the net it went and the net broke with the weight and force of the heavy ball which went straight through, to be stopped by a small boy behind. The Ref, who was in mid-field, gave a goal kick, maintaining that the ball was wide of the post. Pandemonium broke out as the Ashton and Sedgeberrow women supporters threatened the Ref with umbrellas and sticks. Happy Annie went hysterical but the Ref was adamant and Stodge mended the net with a piece of string out of his pocket saying, 'I'll see there won't be nair another gu through there.' His language was then not exactly drawing room and Harold Pumfrey who, besides being Hon. Sec. kept the churchyard tidy, said, 'Stodge, that's enough of that language in front of ladies.' Stodge replied, primed with cider, 'Yer's the hook [the hook used for putting the nets up] and I'll be gone and besides I've yerd thee swear many a time up in that churchyard.' Stodge was a great character but was not of our village. I remember a hurdy-gurdy man playing outside the village cross when Stodge was mowing. I said, 'What do you think of the music?' Stodge replied, 'It's all right but I'd sooner have it along with my fittle.'

The day of the big match on the Wynch which I have just described drew a large crowd for a village—they came by all means of transport and approached the ground through our horse road, past the granary and cow-shed. The date was November 9th and my sister's birthday was on Armistice Day the following Monday, November 11th. Our cowman, dear old George Jinks, was milking seventeen cows and ten weaned calves lay in the bay of the barn. The store cattle had not yet been brought into the yards for the winter and were way up Bredon on Great Hill and in the Leasows. George was a Chapel man, played his melodion (always Sankey Hymns) under the Nine Square apple tree in the garden of his thatched cottage and was always humble and kind, patient with animals and children. He was short and stocky but not all that strong. He told me how his father had carried two sacks of wheat—four hundredweight and a half—up our granary steps for a bet and ruptured himself. At about eight o'clock on the morning of November 11th, George, who had brought the cows in and milked them, coming into our yard from Didcot Ham by way of Gipsies' Lane, turned up at our back door. I had not by then gone to catch the train for school and I answered the door. 'Is

the Master at home, Fred?' he said with a forlorn look in his
eye. 'Yes, Mr. Jinks, I'll fetch him ... Dad, Mr. Jinks wants a
word with you—he looks worried.'

Clearing his throat, Dad went to the door expecting George
to ask him to get a hay seed out of a calf's eye (Dad was very
good at that) or to order some more cattle cake from Gloucester,
or send a telegram to Birmingham for more milk churns. But it
was nothing of the kind. 'Master Archer,' George began, 'some
of the cows be gone off thur fittle and two of um be lame.' I
followed the two anxious-looking men to the lidded place at the
end of the barn where Peasbrook, Spider, Ada and Cherry were
standing tied up, blowing over their morning food of chaff cake
and oat flour. Spider was lame and was licking her front feet,
her lips quite swollen and unable to eat. We had just been put
on the phone, our number being 4, but we had an extension to
Mr. Carter's at the other farm. Dad turned the little handle on
the phone extension and as I listened I heard these words,
'Harry, I'm afraid we've got the Foot and Mouth. I'm just
going to ring Mr. Hastilow the vet and I've told George not to
turn the cows out. Perhaps it would be best if you didn't come
up, as the bull and one or two in-calf cows are in your yard.'
Mr. Hastilow had sent for the Ministry vets and the police by
the time I caught the ten to nine train to school. When I arrived
home that November evening off the four-ten at our station, a
policeman stopped me from taking a short cut through the
yard. Foot and Mouth had been confirmed. Notices were everywhere and in our kitchen Ministry officials were drinking tea
with police officers as darkness fell on this unforgettable scene.
Our local P.C. Smith stayed all night to see that all the animals
were kept in quarantine. George fed the calves in the barn for
the last time and took a kerf or two of hay to the cows in the
long shed who had not got Foot and Mouth but were contacts.
He dipped his heavy boots and leggings well into a bucket of
disinfectant at our courtyard gate and went home to tea a heart-
broken man.

Early next morning valuers arrived to value the stock. Some
of the animals were looking, as George said, 'As if their backs
was as high as St. Pauls Cathedral'; they were most uncomfort-
able, both through want of food which they were unable to eat

and the pain from their feet and ulcerated mouths which were dripping saliva.

Jack Bradfield had been sent to Beckford station for a ton of best coal and Walt was hauling logs of wood from the woodpile in the rickyard into the far end of our back garden to burn the cows after they had been shot. Spot, a brown and white Shorthorn giving five and a half gallons a day—a lot in those days—was George's favourite. When George had been short of churns, Jack Bradfield who helped George teased him, 'I don't know whatever we be a guain to do of all this milk, Jack lad.'

'Dig a hole and put it in, George,' Jack would answer.

'Don't thee talk so dall silly amongst all this work,' and George, as he always did, added: 'You know, Jack, I don't know whatever the Gaffer ud do without this milk money. Thee have a look round the farm, thur yunt much else a comin in.'

But this Tuesday morning, no one from the ploughboys to Dad and Mr. Carter was in any mood for joking. I had a bit of a cold and stayed away from school but was not allowed in the farmyard. At about eleven o'clock the men arrived with their humane killers. What a picture of misery I remember! The ten weaned calves in the barn were killed and dressed first. Liver has always been a tempting dish for me—fried with bacon—and Dad, the policeman and I had calves' liver for breakfast. The calves which had been in contact with the cows were destined to be killed and burnt with the cows. Shepherd Corbisley was a handy butcher and he was helped by tall, lean Arthur Ballard, an Evesham man who had walked our village streets many a night before he came to live in Ashton and work for Mr. Carter and Dad. You see, Arthur was, or had been, a true to type Bredon Hill poacher. At five o'clock in the morning a nice veal calf helped by the Shepherd and Arthur found its way into the old thatched sheep barn adjoining Arthur's cottage. The Shepherd killed and dressed the veal calf, saving it from cremation. Arthur and the Shepherd enjoyed the veal and I was ignorant of the fact until years later. What exactly was going through the mind of George Jinks, our cowman? George had experienced setbacks in the past; we once lost a cow with anthrax; the occasional one developed garget or mastitis for which, in those days before antibiotics were available, little could be done; a calf would die of the dreaded white scour and Joker the bull frequently got loose at night. He had a habit of slipping the chain off from around his neck. George put this right by fixing a leather washer on the tee piece which went through the ring on the chain, but not before one memorable night when Joker escaped.

Mrs. Pickford, a widow, and her two daughters lived in a stone farmhouse below us, between our house and Mr. Carter's where Joker was kept. In front of her small garden was an iron fence of arrow-head railing and Joker managed to slip his nose ring over one of these arrow heads and was stuck there bawling all night just under Mrs. Pickford's window. As she drew aside the bedroom curtains she could just discern the white face of Joker the Hereford in the bright moonlight.

But George Jinks was remembering none of these things this dull November morning. To think that Spot, his pride and joy, had got to be sacrificed when she had not even got the disease. But she was a contact, and the Ministry said she had to go with the rest. Just before the first cow was shot in our back garden, George came to our window with tears making little rivulets down his sun-tanned old face, trickling down through the grey stubble—some dripping from his chin and others from the end of his rather pointed nose. Seeing George crying shook me—a small boy still at Prep school. 'Master Archer,' he began, 'I can't stop here and see this lot, do you think I could go home?'

Dad said, 'We'll manage, George, you go home. I understand.'

George had reared most of the seventeen cows from calves and he knew them all by name and they knew him. Now he went home for the last time. He died some time after with a broken heart. I used to see him in the garden and he told me of years long ago, before the slaughter of animals with Foot and Mouth became law, and how in Squire Bosworth's time the cowmen kept the animals alive by feeding sloppy bran mashes to them. 'It's different now,' George said, 'we be ruled by officials from London.' He struck up another tune on his melodion— 'Dare to be a Daniel, dare to stand alone.'

The slaughter and the burning meant a deal of work. As each cow went down from the humane killer, the next, smelling the blood, hesitated by the granary steps and some had to be forced to the place of execution between the granary and the horse pond, to be brought back afterwards by Turpin, a strong shire horse, who didn't seem to relish his morning's task. A tow chain was placed around each cow's horns and Turpin dragged it to the fire, now burning brightly and stoked by fireman Davis, an old steam-plough driver.

You may wonder how I saw all this sad spectacle as police had forbidden me in the yard. These were the days before any form of indoor sanitation and our privy was just at the end of a row of nut bushes in our back garden—very near to the funeral pyre. It was a two-seater earth closet and I well remember the almanack on the blue-washed wall. An almanack was a must in those places. The page for November had a picture and underneath I read these words, 'Lead Kindly Light amidst Encircling gloom. Lead thou me on.' The picture was of some poor lost soul groping through the darkness of a winter's night. Some of the daymen were busy with spades digging a trench around the rectangular-shaped fire to catch the gravy which poured from these unfortunate beasts. I was sent up the village that evening to buy a can of milk from another farmer. We had never bought milk before and as I came down our village street carrying the milk in the can I caught the smell of that giant barbecue in our back garden and saw the ghostlike figures of men working, keeping the fire burning with more wood and coal and an occasional dash of paraffin.

After much iffing and offing by Ministry vets, Joker the bull at Mr. Carter's was reprieved. So also was Joker's mother, Granny, a pure-bred Hereford who had seen more Christmas Days than I had. She and a few more dry cows were blissfully ignorant of all that was happening to the milkers at Stanley Farm. They were a mile away in the Long Dewrest.

The ashes were still hot after a fortnight and I helped Dad one Saturday afternoon scatter some around our rose trees in the front garden. In all the tragedies of human life, this may sound very unimportant—the premature death of twenty-seven animals. What was the loss really? The Government of the day paid the value of the cows as they were, looking anything but their best; George Jinks never returned to work; Mr. Carter and

Dad, by visiting farm sales after the infection had passed, bought more cows but never had a little herd to compare with the one George Jinks selected and reared.

There was a lot of speculation about how the disease had reached our farm. Some said some of the football crowd brought it with them. Others thought it was the starlings who came in droves every morning to feed on the asparagus berries, now crimson and ripe along the Beckford Way. Shepherd Corbisley, who was up before most of the men, saw a dog fox run through the cows in Didcot Ham early on the Saturday morning, the morning of the football match. At school that week Miss Morris was teaching us about the plague of London and the subsequent fire. I thought of Spot, and George who the week before had made music in the bottom of a three-gallon milk bucket as he sat on a greasy three-legged stool and told me as the froth came almost to the top that he 'was drawing the blessing'.

'I'll be dalled if this yunt the best cow we've had since I a bin yur,' he said as he gave her an extra bowl of linseed cake. Then George had told me how 'the Master allus made me milk Granny separate when you was a babby and I called her the "Babby's cow".' A part of her milk was kept to rear me, so I had a little thing in common with Joker.

CHAPTER EIGHT

COUNTRY WOMEN OF THE 1920s

FRANK WHEATCROFT, that man of so many parts and with experience in all matters, loved above all to talk to me about women. 'I wishes as how I was a young man agun and knowed as much about life as I do now, but that yunt possible,' he told me. 'What's that song as we yurs on the wireless, Frederick? [he'd just got a crystal set] Madam et Mobilley?' 'Madonna Mobile,' I suggested. 'That's it,' Frank replied, spitting on his hands ready to pull a bit more mould up to the early potatoes with his twelve-inch-bladed hoe. 'I knows what it myums, mind tha,' he said. 'It myums that women be fickle minded—you never knows when you a got em. When tha bist married, thee ul understand. One day you can get away with murder amus, another day you can't get away with it—can't do a thing right for em. Mind, they suffers but thee bisn't hardly old enough to understand that, but you a got to umor them at times, hold the candle to um. If I could see my time over again I'd marry the same ooman. Mind, when they be in the right umor they ud amus ut ya. Mind when you marries you ties a knot with your tongue as you can't undo with your teeth; it's a life sentence. I'm a warnin' you—be careful.' He gave one or two more drags with his hoe up the potato row and went towards the shed. 'That ul do for tonight, it's the wrong end of the day for any more, thur's always tomorrow. I was always told afore I married,' he went on, 'Marry a big ooman and get a little house and you won't have to buy much furniture. That's a rum un' ain't it? When you salts a pig for bacon, never let a ooman touch it, it ul go bad else.' These were his final words of wisdom: 'Women be funny craters, that's the sartin truth, Frederick, they be fickle-minded.'

I have already mentioned Mildred and her sweethearting along with Humphrey, the young Squire. Her stockbroker father knew full well that the sooner he could get her off his hands the better. A wedding was arranged in Cheltenham.

Humphrey was dragged out of the smokeroom of one of the best hotels only minutes before the time for the wedding service. The best man found him in the Double Gloucester half seas over. After the ceremony when Humphrey was due to take Mildred to the station to catch the Bournemouth train, the best man looked inside Humphrey's suitcase to make sure that he had packed everything. What he found there didn't seem at all suitable for a Bournemouth honeymoon in high summer—there were a pair of hobnail boots and two Oxford shirts.

The best man, who knew Mildred (who didn't?), said, 'You're expecting some heavy going, Humphrey, and you a hunting man as well.' Mildred smiled, she had no illusions about men. Tom Wheatcroft cleared his throat as he told me in a whisper: 'You know, Frederick, a regiment of soldiers udn't be too many men for her, her's forrad, very forrad. I a sin things in the nag stable as I udn't like to tell a young innocent chap like you.'

I said, 'Tom, when I biked back from school at Evesham one day in the hot summer of '26 she told me as we cycled up Sedgeberrow Bank as it was so hot she hadn't put any knickers on.'

'The wicked ooman, course you was but a small boy but that's how her tempted. Have you seen her in the winter with that fine fur coat?'

'Oh the squirrel one?'

'That's it,' he said. 'You knows what they says round yur, I think I ought to tell you—fur coat, no drawers.'

Mildred's husband drank himself to death; Tom said he 'abused himself'. Mildred became known as the Merry Widow and her admirers came by pony and trap, some in cars. One, Gordon Hampton, from the other side of Evesham, died suddenly and Mildred, according to Frank Wheatcroft, dropped a lovely red rose on his coffin and said these words: 'There, that's the only man that's been any good for me.' Bill Bosworth was taken ill and Doctor Overthrow told him straight that he had overdone his nature along with Mildred. Apart from her passion for men, Mildred had been a trained nurse and did a lot of good in our village, helping the poor, who often had large families, when there was sickness in the house.

CHAPTER NINE

SHOPPY BRADFIELD

SHOPPY BRADFIELD got her name from her occupation of keeping the village shop. This shop had closed before I was born and she had lost her husband. He was gamekeeper for the eccentric old Squire and Old Herbert, Shoppy's husband, had to report on anything he had seen in Ashton Big Wood during each day. Some days he had poachers, others deer that had escaped from the nearby park. One day he told the Squire that he had seen a cock pheasant cohabiting with a hen—But back to Shoppy. She kept fowls in the cider apple orchard opposite her brick and tiled Victorian cottage. She was a little, stout woman, bad on her feet, with eyes like saucers. Some called her 'Mrs. Egg Bradfield' and I thought it was because of her eyes being like eggs, but no, she kept a nice lot of Rhode Island fowls wired in her orchard and collected the eggs in a peck wicker basket twice a day. By Friday she had enough eggs to take to Evesham and sell in the market. She had a large, old-fashioned basinette—a sort of glorified pram; this she loaded with wicker baskets full of eggs and limped past our house on the way to the station to catch the eight-fifty a.m. train to Evesham. I travelled on that train and the baskets full of eggs were loaded into the guard's van together with the basinette, and Shoppy, dressed in her best hat trimmed by herself and wearing an extra coat, black gloves and lace-up boots, often came into our carriage. Apart from her poultry, she visited furniture sales and had an eye for a bargain. She raised money in all sorts of ways in aid of the local chapel, but how do I remember her best of all? One hears of the May Queen and the Gipsy Queen, but Shoppy was known as 'The Brawn Queen'. She bought pigs' heads and in her copper boiler at the back of the cottage she made a quantity of brawn. She must have owned dozens of basins for she trusted the buyers of this brawn to bring back their empties. I never tasted it—there was usually enough pig offal around our household every winter. George thrived on it for his lunch when he worked for us, bringing great hunks of it to eat with his bread and cheese. Then one day he told me, 'I've had enough of Shoppy's brawn, the last basin had a rim of rice pudding about an inch above the brawn.'

CHAPTER TEN

COW DOCTORS AND THEIR ANCIENT REMEDIES

I SUPPOSE the doctoring of sick animals has gone on in one way or another for centuries. The people of ancient Egypt had an uncanny knowledge of animal diseases; the Arabs, by mere accident, found out how to tell whether their mares were pregnant. They noticed that where their urine fell on the grass or corn, the crop grew much faster than where other animals grazed. From this they decided they could find out whether their wives or concubines were expecting babies—their urine was used to water pots of grain. These pots were placed alongside others which were watered with the urine from women who had passed the age of childbearing. If the woman was pregnant the corn grew much faster. Considering that this took place thousands of years ago, it brings home once more the fact that there is nothing new under the sun.

Tom Wheatcroft was a cow doctor. Vets were first employed by the Army and it is not so long ago that they only attended horses. Tom had remedies galore; if a cow lost its cud or was unable to bring back its food to ruminate, Tom had a remedy. He drenched it with an evil-smelling mixture. When I say he drenched it, I mean he poured the liquid down its throat with a pint-and-a-half bottle filled over and over again. Drench seems to be the operative word. First of all he boiled a large saucepan full of cabbage and fat bacon which had gone rancid, or 'reasty' as we called it. This was boiled until all the goodness had come out of the cabbage, leaving a green liquid, and the fat from the bacon left a scale of oily substance—a kind of scum on the top. After straining through a colander, the medicine was allowed to cool to blood heat. Next came the drenching. Can you imagine anything more likely to bring back food than this mixture of boiled bacon and cabbage water? I've helped Tom many times pour this liquid down the cow's throat, accompanied by belches and rumbles. It often worked and the cow would decide to start again that all-important part of her make-up and chew her cud. I think there is nothing so satisfying, so endless to watch, as a cow on a winter's day lying on a bed of straw with a full belly, a contented look on her face, chewing, swallowing, and starting all over again as another lot of half-digested material ejects into her mouth.

Enough of cows and chewing the cud and Tom's remedy of the fat bacon. When we had a cow calve in the loosebox next to the bull-pen, Tom took no risks, especially in winter time. 'Don't thee get giving her a gutsful of that ice-cold water from the pump,' he used to tell me. Tom then took his milking stool, coated with the grease of ages, turned his cap back to front and took a tablespoonful of fresh liquor—lard without salt—in his hand and tenderly applied this to the four quarters of the cow-bag. With his three-gallon bucket between his knees he milked about two gallons of cherry curds or 'beasting', that is the first milking, from the cow, filled the bucket with water and gave her the mixture to drink. 'Lukewarm,' he said, 'it won't be such a shock to her stomach.' The rest of the curds Tom took home to make a pudding. 'Some of the best,' he said.

Tom used to tell me of an outbreak of Foot and Mouth disease 'afore the strictions'. 'We fed the cows on oatmeal pap or gruel and most on um pulled through. Mind tha, they went terribly poor and thin, like hurdles, and I never cared a lot about looking after screws. Linseed cake was cheap and we bunged plenty a that into um when they begun to ut. Never wants to see it again though.'

'Where does this Foot and Mouth come from, Tom?' I said.

'Bless thee, bwoy, it's them droves a starlings as takes it from one farm to another. Course,' he said, 'I saw the lot; anthrax is the quickest and the wust. I expect you remembers that roan we had, old Ada. Well, when her died I started skinning ready for the nacker and thee Dad sent for the vet from Asum and he said it was anthrax. If ever I'd nicked my finger with the knife, I'd a bin a stiff un along of her. Fred, my bwoy, when you starts to shave, I suppose that won't be long now, pay a few extra coppers and get thyself a good brush—guaranteed pure badger hair and free from anthrax. Them foreigners unt particular what sort o' hair they put in brushes so I'm a tellin ya.'

Next holiday I brought Old Tom back one of these brushes

warranted pure bristle.

'That is good on ya,' he said. 'Mine was amus wore down to the handle.'

Tom had reared more calves than folks you would see watching Cheltenham Town play football on a Boxing Day. He had his ways with what he called 'scour' or white diarrhoea. For scour, Tom was a believer in water straight from the spring, then he dosed them with what he called 'puff-who powders', blowing them from the packets down their throats. If this failed he used raw eggshells, powdered chalk and peppermint. Tom was often successful with calves and their ailments and when we turned out the weaners at four or five months old about May Day when the grass was a bit lush, Tom threaded a short piece of tarred string through each one's brisket with his penknife—an old wives' tale, you may say, but it was supposed to be a preventative against blackleg or murrain. I only remember losing one calf from this ailment—a black and white half-bred Hereford, as fat as a snail and as slick as a mole. It lay bloated under the withies and I suspected anthrax, but Tom knew different and after letting the gas out of its distended belly with a shuppuck, both lighting a Woodbine to hide the smell, we buried it. Tom said if she'd had anthrax there would have been blood from the nostrils. 'I told your dad this keep's too good for calves—it'd fatten a bullock avout any cake,' he said.

CHAPTER ELEVEN

THE WAR MEMORIAL

OUR VILLAGE, united in times of hardship, especially the poverty of the late nineteenth century, was also united in times of war. We lost ten good men out of forty-eight who served in the forces in the 1914–18 war. Several were badly wounded and those who suffered most were most loathe to talk about it.

After the peace celebrations with a bonfire and fireworks in the little peaceful village, folk began talking about erecting some permanent memorial in stone to serve as a reminder of those village lads we had lost and who could so ill be spared.

A meeting was held in the school to discuss a site for a land-mark such as we could be proud of. Those of us who have experienced the ups and downs of village life in the early twenties know that divisions just come from nowhere. Two cricket teams had played their matches quite independently for years just because the one team had refused to play a small farmer who scratched a living by Ashton wood from rabbits and blackberries and a few store cattle. These cattle broke out into the President of the cricket club's mowing grass and Hubert the small farmer was banned from playing cricket with the Club. What did Hubert do but start a club on his own which he called the United. Such is the independence of the men of the land. 'Stomachful' Tom Wheatcroft called it, but there has always been that bit of extra under the belt of these men.

The meeting to discuss the War Memorial was, to say the least, tempestuous. This was unfortunate and I shall say at the beginning that there were faults on both sides. The new owner of the Croft had a spinney of larch, silver birch and chestnut near his garage on the boundary of his property. This had been enclosed many years ago by the previous owner—a financier named Saunderson—and added to the Croft. The new owner was known by everyone as 'the Old Gentleman' and he from the kindness of his heart offered the village his small spinney oppo-site the school as a site for the memorial.

'It yunt his to give,' said Gunner Wood who was still smarting from his wounds, the effects of poison gas and two years in a German prison camp. 'That land belongs to the village. It's the old pound and our old chap can mind the time when stray cattle and sheep were impounded there, afore old Saunderson pinched it. Yunt that right, Ernest?' he said to Ernest Bradfield who was sitting by him. 'It's the sartin truth,' Ernest agreed.

This really started the trouble about where the memorial should be put. The natives resented the fact that the Old Gentleman was giving away something that really belonged to the village. After much discussion the village doctor in the chair tried to get a decision. 'At the Cross where we all goes to worship,' said Sarah Jones. 'In Attwood's orchard,' said Joe Baker. 'In the corner of Tom Archer's rickyard,' said Pedlar Mason from the hamlet of Paris in a fold of Bredon Hill.

The doctor said the answer was a ballot and a date was chosen to hold this in the school. By an overwhelming majority the supporters of the Pound won the election.

'We won't be done,' said Joe Baker, who had lost a son in France. Ernest Bradfield had, as Tom said, 'bin further afield'— Salonika, and that was where he said the war was won.

Ernest was a fine figure of a man who wore a black bowler on Armistice Days, marching slightly ahead, shoulders forward and body upright which gave a waltzing effect as he followed the ex-Service men and the Tewkesbury band playing the one and only Colonel Bogey. The row of medals across his broad chest were about the maximum that the lapel of his coat would carry and they swayed and jingled like a martingale on some great horse pulling a brewer's dray.

For weeks after the meeting, the money had been pouring in to pay for the Portland stone cross to be erected in the Pound. The Opposition had held their meetings at the full moon with Pedlar Mason as their leader.

One did not hear the word communist used in those days in the early twenties; extremists were known as Bolshi agitators. Pedlar was one of them. He liked to stir up things. His only son had been gassed on the Western Front and developed T.B. and Pedlar was understandably bitter; he had no time for King and Country, in fact the only one he had time for was Pedlar.

A certain plasterer, one Sapper Allen, was a fellow traveller with the anti-Pound mob. Sapper was a master of his craft and did much work on Tewkesbury Abbey and later at Stratford Theatre. Pedlar was continually making cracks at the Old Gentleman, the doctor, Geordie Hime the artist, Percy Gamble a retired engineer and all the upper crust of our village who supported the Pound site. He composed poetry of a sort and stuck his efforts on Stocky Hill's front door, which was never opened, and on the two elm trees in the hedgerow of our rickyard. The raising of the money and the planning of the memorial all took time and Pedlar was trying to put a question mark in people's minds. 'He'll end up in clink [Gloucester Jail] as sure as hell's a mouse-trap,' said the quiet, deep thinking Shepherd Marsh, but Pedlar knew just how far to go.

With very little support Sapper Allen set to and started a rival memorial in his yard just in front of his barn and behind the two reconstructed stone balls which he had made as an ornament to the front gate-posts of his cottage. This Memorial was a masterpiece, it just grew from a square base—first one step and then the next, all done in cement and granite chippings, trowelled and dowelled, skimmed and floated. The *pièce de résistance* was a laurel wreath which wound round the upright pillar, like a boa constrictor. The top was finished by a cross and he covered it with a Union Jack.

Speculation grew to fever pitch as the money had almost been raised to erect the official memorial in the Pound and a Cheltenham builder had been commissioned to make a sound job of it. It was Whitsuntide and the weather was ideal for the early haymaking and, most important, for our annual Whit Monday cricket match against Alcester and Ragley Park. This was an all-day match; the Old Gentleman gave a salad lunch to all who wished to attend and, needless to say, most of the villagers were there. I stayed for lunch but came home for tea so that I could help Tom Wheatcroft, our cowman, suckle the calves and tell him the score.

'Frederick, I s'pose thee hast noticed what's gwain on on the village green by the cross?' he said.

'No, Tom, I came the yard way,' I said.

'Well, thee pop across the rickyard and have a look. Dalled if

I knows what thee father and them gentlemen down at the match ul say when stumps be drawn.' I went and looked between the two giant elms. The hawthorn was gone out of blow and the elder, or ellun, gave out that intoxicating scent. There, in the middle of the green, were a group of enthusiastic, sincere men, stripped to their striped Oxford shirts, making the concrete foundation for Sapper's memorial. Not if I live to be a hundred shall I see such an act of sheer audacity being done with such precise timing as on that day of the all-day match between Ashton and Alcester and Ragley Park. A square of well made concrete, mixed by Ernest, Joe, Pedlar Mason and Gunner Wood, was being levelled by Sapper Allen with his plasterer's trowel and spirit level. It set as hard as 'the devil's backside' said Old Stoge, our roadman.

The Council stepped in the next day and gave an order that no more building was to be done on the green. Stoge was ordered to break the concrete, but Sapper had put something in the mixture which defied Stoge's pickaxe and it remained covered with soil and grass for many years until the signpost was erected. During hot dry summers the square brown patch still showed in the midst of our village green, and Sunday dinner times when Sapper was primed to the full and smoking his cherry pipe which held almost half an ounce of twist tobacco, he would click his heels together, remove his cap and give a solemn salute where his memorial might have been. Then as he wended his way around the many corners of Gypsies' Lane he sang Tipperary and shouted to us boys in a kind of pidgin French. Sapper's gone now, but he did try.

Pedlar died of what was called smoker's cough. I well remember the problem of bringing his body across the fields from Paris. The shortest route led through our rickyard and that's the way he would have come but for one reason. There was no public footpath through the rickyard, although it was used often by the people of Paris. An ancient idea still existed that where a corpse was carried, it automatically became a right of way. Dad and his partner were dubious about this and persuaded the people concerned to wheel Pedlar on the four-wheeled bier fetched by Ponto from Beckford down the official path past the Tythe Court barn. Such was life and death in those times.

Back to the official Memorial. On November 8th, 1924, our local Journal reported the scene. The Cornish Cross with a sword pointing downwards upon a pedestal and steps, all done in Portland Stone by the real masters of this work—Messrs. Martins of Cheltenham—was unveiled by that distinguished soldier from the neighbouring parish of Elmley Castle, General Sir Francis Davies, K.C.B., K.C.M.G., K.C.V.O.

My father was among several villagers who welcomed the General. The inscription was on one side with the names of the fallen carved underneath. On the other side we read these words which I think explain everything that happened in those grim years: 'These were a wall unto us, both by night and day.'

The General impressed on us all to tell future generations what this all stood for and added it would be a pity if a stranger entered our village in a hundred years' time and enquired about this stone and none of the villagers knew. It was sad that the little group who favoured Sapper's memorial refused to have their relations' names put on this memorial; later they relented and we can only say: 'God bless them, every one.'

CHAPTER TWELVE

HAPPY NANCY

HAPPY NANCY, who lived when I was a boy in an old thatched cottage along with Jack Plumbley, had come from a well-to-do family but she just took to drink and went to pieces. Her cottage lay alongside the footpath to the hamlet of Grafton and what she had in common with Jack I could never fathom out. She had been brought up a lady and Jack was plain uncouth—they did both drink cider, I suppose that was it.

Nancy took long walks alone around the perimeter of our hill, visiting pubs from Elmley Castle on the north side to Overbury on the south side. She would set off after tea carrying her walking stick and arrive at her destination ready for opening time and stay until the pub closed. She knew the short cuts home, the footpaths, the stiles, the streams, and she never travelled on the hard road.

One moonlight night in winter, she had been Overbury way and was taking the footpath which ran by Beckford Coppice and the two cottages at Cobblers. Joe Wheatcroft (no relation to the Ashton Wheatcrofts) lived in one cottage. Joe was game-keeper for a retired Army Officer who farmed that part of the hill. A real character, expert in all the wiles of trapping rabbits, stalking both birds and beasts that preyed on his pheasants which he reared in the paddock by his house. Joe told me this himself as he half sat, half lay on his Victorian sofa one summer evening. 'Have you ever seen a bald-headed woman in the moonlight, Master Archer?' he asked. 'No,' I said, 'I've seen lots of things in the moonlight but nothing like that. Have you, Joe?' I was itching to hear his story. Joe's eyes sparkled, he moistened his lips with his tongue, knocked his pipe out on the hob of the kitchen range and took a sup from a mug of cider he had on a little table by the side of the sofa. 'I don't believe in ghosts,' Joe chuckled, 'and I have walked this hill of a night time these forty years, but this particular night me and the missus was abed, it was turned eleven, and I heard a squeal in the coppice like a vixen—you've heard um no doubt, Master

Archer. Well, I said to the missus, that vixen sounds almost human. Then I heard a woman's voice crying "Help!" I sat up in bed, lit the candle, went downstairs and then lit my lantern. When I took the path towards the coppice which followed the stream, I heard the cries and squeals getting louder. As I lifted my lantern,' Joe continued, 'a figure loomed in front of me —a bald-headed woman screaming. My hair stood on end, lifting my cap about two inches off my head as I stood dumbfounded. It was Happy Nancy from Ashton.'

'What was she up to at that time of night?'

'That's just what I was goin' to tell you. Her had lost her wig and her had lost her way.'

'But, Joe,' I said, 'who would have thought she had a wig? Her hair was in auburn curls.'

'Well, her have, Master Archer, and I found him after a while. You see, the wig fell into the stream as she crossed it and it floated towards my place, and after a bit of a struggle, I rescued the wig with her walking stick out of the drinking trough by my back door.'

'What did you do then?' I asked. 'You didn't just leave her?'

'No, by this time the blood had come back into my veins and I took her down to the stile, helped her over and put her on the footpath to Ashton.' Joe added with a wry smile: '1914–18 poked the breeze up me a time or two but I've never bin frit so much as that night Happy Nancy got lost. I wish you ud keep her at Ashton, Master Archer.'

'Sometimes she causes a stir at our village,' I told Joe. 'The drink affects her but people understand. Last Armistice service at the memorial, she was standing with some more of the village women, a bit unsteady like, and you know the grassy bank that slopes down to the road quite steeply?'

Joe said, 'Oi, I recollects.'

'Well, all at once she lost her sway, as they say in the village, and rolled down to the bottom of the bank finishing upside down in the road and she showed a fair bit of red flannel petticoat.'

'You means her went ass over ud,' Joe added.

'Pitchpole,' I would have said, but Joe was a generation before me.

CHAPTER THIRTEEN

A FÊTE IN THE 1920s

WHEN MONEY had to be raised in our village, the committee (we loved forming committees) decided on a fête. The locals never did understand the circumflex e and these functions were known as 'feets'. 'Bist a goin to the feet?' old Frank Wheatcroft would ask me as I walked up the Groaten from the four-ten train from school, which stopped at our station on the little branch line. 'It's tomorrow, Saturday, as ever was,' he went on, 'and Sir James is opening it from the cricket pavilion.'

'I know, Frank, I've got to present him with a button-hole—carnations, I think.'

'Well, thee ul manage that bit of a job surely?' he said.

That Friday evening the cricket ground was a hive of activity. The fête was for the Cricket Club. The stalls were both numerous and varied. The evergreen hoop-la was being erected, a stall was run by a buxom farmer's wife, Maud Handy, whose son had already been through all the cigarette packets (some of the prizes) and taken out the fag cards. This gave him an unfair advantage over me. Another circular tent top of pink and white covered a table stacked with toys, trinkets and all the odd sort of things people give for these affairs. Every parcel had a long string on it which reached outside the stall. 'Bunty pulls the string' was placarded on cardboard on the top of the tent pole. By paying threepence or sixpence you were allowed to pull the string and as the showman said 'a prize every time, lady'.

Mrs. Hunter, part gipsy, one of the travelling type, had brought her donkeys over from the other side of the hill and donkey rides for children at sixpence a time were to be had alongside the wire fence which parted the cricket ground from the Naits. The Naits had not been mown and the mowing grass here was rank and tall with meadowsweet and cow parsley. Saturday morning, after the mist along the brookside and a drenching dew on the grass, promised to be hot and fine and we were not to be disappointed. A horse and dray of Howard

Cambridge's was being driven by his carter, old Jimmy Blizzard. He was loaded with trestles and tables for the teas, then he fetched the coconut shy stuff to be erected against the back of an old cowshed where the horse-drawn cricket roller and mower were kept. Howard Cambridge had an idea that, to be different, we would throw rick pegs at the coconuts instead of the usual balls; this proved quite successful, the coconuts falling more by luck than judgment. By three o'clock everyone was assembled by the pavilion. The Ashton Cricket Club flag—yellow and navy, the same colours as the football team jerseys (the Tigers)—was fluttering in the slight breeze. Sir James and Lady Cosnett were both on the steps for the opening ceremony, supported by Mr. Cambridge, senior, the Vicar and, in fact, all the upper class we could muster. Sir James was a very ordinary sort of man, 'No side on him,' Tom Wheatcroft confided to me, 'thee hast no cause to be nervous of him, nor his missus, they be just like one a we.' Edna Collins was about a year younger than me and she had been chosen to present Lady Cosnett with a bouquet as soon as the fête was officially opened. Edna—shortish, plump with puppy fat—walked up as gracefully as she could in her pink crêpe de Chine dress ornamented with rosebuds, curtsied and gave her bouquet to Lady Bosnett. Then came my turn just as the clapping died down for Edna. I had been smartened up no end by Mother and had plastered Jockey Club on my then fair hair which actually had a parting. As I gave Sir James his buttonhole, expecting to make a hasty retreat, he grabbed me by the hand and said what a smart young fellow I was and hoped that one day I would be playing for the village team (this I did some years later). The fête was under way.

A railway ganger who was staying in the next village brought with him a 'shocking coil'—an electrical device that sent pins and needles up the arm by holding the two terminals from the battery and which was supposed to cure rheumatism. He placed the two leads in a bucket of water, put half a crown in the bottom and charged twopence a go to get the half crown. I saw lots of people in all sorts of contortions but the electric shock in the water just wouldn't allow time to grab the half crown. As I stood there about tea-time, a youth, Jim Bradfield, had a go and much to everyone's delight retrieved the half-crown. It is sur-

prising how ingenious people can get when they put heart and
soul into an effort to raise money for a good cause. Howard
Cambridge gave one of his best weaner pigs for a competition.
The people who took part had to nurse the pig, keep it quiet
and sing a song in front of the crowd without laughing. One
after another tried and the pig squealed and the crowd laughed
and the competitors, laughing themselves, gave up. Mrs. Hunter
had gypsy blood in her. She was game to make an honest copper
as she said. She nursed the pig in her apron, stood on the
pavilion steps and gently rocked it until it was almost sleeping
and sang as she rocked the young pig like nursing a baby—

'The tears rolled down her sun burnt cheeks,
And dropped on the letter in her hand.
Is it true, too true, more trouble in our native land . . .'

She sang without batting an eyelid. She looked dead serious as
the pig was spending a penny, soaking her apron and running
onto the green grass at the foot of the steps. The crowd were
almost hysterical with laughter. Mrs. Hunter won the pig—she
won other pigs at other fêtes—and deserved it.

At every fête someone has to tell fortunes. Evangeline Agg, a
farmer's daughter ('a fine piece', Frank described her. 'Her looks
all right when 'ers got up for fox hunting, mind'), pitched her
tent under the withies not far from where Fred Parminter was
boiling the water in a copper for the tea. We helped Fred to
gather wood to stoke the copper boiler and the ladies made the
tea.

Evangeline was dressed as a gypsy. This was not awfully difficult; she had raven black hair, about thirtyish, Frank reckoned
she was, and she had a sort of olive complexion. She wore a
coloured scarf over her head, two enormous earrings, bangles
and no stockings which Frank said made her a bit gallus. From
the bottom of her red dressing-gown affair, she showed a pair of
fancy garters. Two chairs were placed either side of the table in
the tent and a crystal ball shone like a diamond on the green
baize of the card table. She did very good business all day. 'I be
goin' to have me bob's worth,' old Frank told me, 'if it's only to
hold hands with her for a few minutes.' We boys peeped under

the canvas and listened to what she told her clients.

The sun had gone down over Bredon Hill, the dew was rising and most of us were gone home, but Frank Wheatcroft had to stay to help Jimmy Blizzard load the trestle tables and clear up the stalls, the next day being Sunday. 'Thee ut remember Evangeline a forchun telling,' he asked me on the Monday morning.

'Yes, what about it? She did very well for the club, didn't she?'

'Oi her did,' Frank said, 'and her didn't do so bad after the feet.'

'What happened, Frank? Nothing bad, I hope?'

'Well, yes and no,' Frank said. 'You remember young Roland from Beckford a comin' about tay time?'

'Yes,' I said.

'Well,' said Frank, 'this is the sarten truth as I be tellin' ya. Me and Jimmy had a squint in that tent just at the edge a night, so to speak, and Master Roland was telling Evangeline's fortune in there. If thee dostn't know what I means you ul one day.'

I had a good idea what Frank meant. He talked in riddles but it was a thing that we all got used to.

The fête was a great success, as they usually were, but about a fortnight after I had been helping Tom Wheatcroft to move some weaner calves from the long shed into the lidded place and I caught ringworm off them—one on my arm and another in the parting of my hair. Nothing unusual, you may say, but, and it was a big but, Edna Collins started ringworm at the same time. Didn't old Tom tease me! 'What was thee and Edna at in that rank mowing grass full o' meadowsweet? Old Jimmy Blizzard a just told me that when he mowed it, it was beat down terrible by the fence t'other side of the coconut shies, some young uns had bin a rompin' there. It's no good saying it wasn't thee and Edna, Frederick, cos you was sin.' That took a long time to live down.

CHAPTER FOURTEEN

THE SPROUT-PICKING CHAMPIONSHIP

ALL THE old farmers I ever met said it was Lloyd George who let them down after the 1914 war. Somebody had to have the blame and in the early twenties everything slumped in price, especially corn. Some farmers just let their land tumble down to grass, not having the spirit to sow leys; others went in for market gardening. This industry had been mostly confined to the Evesham vales—good early land—but sprouts and peas grew quite well in our village and some farmers grew a fair acreage of sprouts, others let fields to the more experienced Evesham growers. Dad and his partner were one step ahead of the local farmers; they had been growing sprouts and other market crops in a big way since about 1907. They had developed an excellent strain of brussels sprouts by selecting stems of their own and growing their own seed on top of Bredon Hill, miles away from any other green stuff, which was important to prevent cross fertilisation by bees. Archer and Carter's strain was locally famous. Where you have a good article and a good name in the market, good workmen are a must. Both Dad and Mr. Carter were most particular about the growing and picking of sprouts; the plants had to be firm, the ground had to be just right. A teaspoonful of sulphate of ammonia was put close to each plant when the plants started growing; close to each plant meant that the backs of the men were almost bent double as the white sugary sulphate was dribbled through the hand almost touching the ground. If the fertiliser fell on the plant it scorched it and if it fell a foot away the fibrous roots of the plant could not reach it.

Picking sprouts has changed a lot over the last sixty years. The old pickers packed forty pounds into the bags or wicker hampers; then, in the twenties, Mr. Bernard Nicklin, an Ashton man, invented the sprout net to hold twenty pounds. He bought secondhand fish netting from Lowestoft, the women in his packing shed cut this into squares and a cottage industry developed in our village as both men and women wove these squares of netting with soft string into net containers. The advantages of the net were that the sprouts could be seen by the buyer, they kept in good condition with plenty of air and they looked much more of an attractive pack than a forty-pound hamper. The industry continued for a while until it was taken over by the fish netting manufacturers who continue to make twenty-pound sprout nets today.

We had several pickers who could pick sixty nets a day piece work, but George was the Maestro. He had long fingers, a strong wrist and with his fingers moving all the time he was easily the fastest sprout picker in the district. Have you noticed that so often the man who is fastest at his work is also the best workman? George was a fast picker and a clean picker, all the yellow leaves and bits of stem slipped through his fingers and fell to the ground and the hard button sprouts dropped into the nets. His nets filled with remarkable speed and every so often one of George's clenched fists pushed the sprouts down into the very corners of the nets and made the pack easy to see and much more attractive to look at. It's hard to work up much enthusiasm about sprout picking; conditions are wet, cold and frosty at that time of the year and a field of sprouts with white hoar frost covering it does not look very inviting at about seven-thirty on a winter's day.

One January we had a piece of sprouts on some land rented for the year from a local farmer who had done the ground well, sheeping off turnips the year before. Dad and Mr. Carter gave it a good supply of meat and bone manure and the crop of sprouts was a sight for sore eyes. George started with the rest of the gang picking sprouts into twenty-pound nets as soon as the morning sun peeped over Broadway Hill. Tom Higgins, a local blacksmith, had perfected a sprout net holder—just a simple crate with hooks at each of the four top corners. He and Mr. Nicklin made this especially to take a sprout net stretched wide open for filling. George kept a supply of empty nets under the belt of his coat and as he filled them he left them in a neat row between the sprout stems. Dad came in to dinner at one o'clock, and 'I believe George is going to make history today,' he said. 'I reckon he won't be far short of picking eighty nets by dark at half past four.'

I was itching to know what happened that January afternoon. About a quarter to five Dad drove the Sunbeam tourer
into the yard. He had just helped to load the last of the sprouts
after they had been weighed on the spring balance hung from a
rough tripod of nut sticks on the headland. As he washed in
cold water in our kitchen sink, he said, 'Well, young George
have done it—eighty nets in under eight hours.'

The news went round the village. Some old stagers said it
couldn't be done. 'He never carried um out and weighed um,'
said others, but George did all that and picked them clean. The
local paper got to know about it and published it on the Friday
under the title 'Is this a Record?' followed by the facts about
George. Letters poured in. Some pickers said, 'Oi, and the gaffer
ul expect us all to do it every day and piece-work rates will go
down,' but nothing like that happened. There was only one
George—I've picked with him and worked hard for forty nets
in a day, while George had got sixty by three o'clock.

Some of the Evesham gardeners who were jealous of their
skill at growing vegetables said, 'Let's have a competition and
see who can pick the most sprouts, picked cleanly, in two
hours.' This idea took on and the following year a competition
was held in a large field near Pershore. Publicity was given to
this in the local and national press. The B.B.C. sent Robin
Whitworth down to report; even Beachcomber mentioned it in
his column in humorous vein. Cameramen came to film it for
the cinemas and a silver cup was given by the firm who supplied
us with the fertiliser. 'It's all a stunt,' some of the A'sum crowd
said. 'Just to sell Tom Archer's and Harry Carter's sprout sid.
Did'st see it advertised in the *Journal*?—twenty shillings a
pound mind tha.' We had two wheat sacks full of seed standing
both sides the oven grate in our kitchen and it was part of my
duties to weigh it into pounds and post it to all parts of the
country.

Back to the competition. I went over there early in Mr.
Carter's car with Dad and George. It was a bitter cold morning
in mid-winter. The competition started about ten-thirty and
lasted until twelve-thirty; at nine o'clock, when we arrived on
the field, the sprouts were drooping their leaves with frost and

a fog lay over the vale. We had some lunch and a hot flask of tea and the sun broke through, partly thawing the rime on the sprout leaves. George was like a boxer before the fight, he hopped about from one foot to the other and was raring to go. Harry Claridge was there from the local Bon Marché—a quick-witted character whose adverts in the local paper were gems; Jack Harrison, a local grower, was at the mike and announced: 'Enter unto the field of battle Harry Claridge, the well-known draper from the Bon Marché—his trousers are still coming down.' 'Jack will have his joke,' said Harry to Dad. 'How's that navy blue suit wearing I had made for you?'

Dad said, 'It would have been cheap at half the price, but seriously, Harry, it was the best five-pound suit I've had for years.'

By now the pickers were lined up like athletes about to run a race. Two rows of sprouts each, and behind every picker an important man with 'Steward' printed on a yellow disc fixed to the lapel of his coat. The stewards followed four stems, or to be more exact, four yards behind each picker. If a picker did not clear all the sprouts off each stem, the steward fetched him back to do so. The steward had also to see that no sprouts were thrown on the ground and that no leaves or bits of stem were put in the nets.

George took off his overcoat and then, to our amazement on this bitter cold morning when we had turned up collars and scarves, he took off his jacket too and hung both on the haw-thorn hedge on the headland; there he stood rolling up his sleeves, waistcoated, on that winter day, his large hands trembling a little until the whistle was blown to start the competition. Within minutes George took his first net out of the holder and put in an empty one. The pickers, backs bent, worked down the long field like an army advancing. It was fairly quiet apart from the rustling of the sprout leaves and the cracking of the sprouts as they were pushed off the stems by the palm of the hand. Occasionally we heard a steward fetch back a picker to clear a stem but these men were what was known as everyday sprouters and needed little supervision. After two hours the whistle blew, the sprouts were weighed and each picker had at least one of his nets emptied out onto an empty dray for the judges to scrutinise, looking for leaves and bits of stem and judging the quality of the pack. One man was disqualified for rough picking and George, as we had hoped, won the cup; he picked the most and picked them clean and proved to everyone that he did pick eighty nets in under eight hours the previous January. The cup was presented at a little function in Evesham Town Hall and George broadcast to the nation how to pick sprouts. Harry Claridge's next advertisement in the *Journal* read that the champion sprout picker was wearing a Bon Marché overcoat. Harry also gave him a new one. Since this great day in the little world of sprout pickers, men have topped the hundred mark, picking over one hundred nets in a day; new varieties have been introduced, but in their day Archer and Carter's strain stood supreme.

At the Regal Cinema at Evesham on the Saturday afternoon, we saw George in the newsreel picking sprouts—the King of Sprout-pickers from Ashton.

CHAPTER FIFTEEN

MAXIM AND TART

ABOUT A mile from my house towards the foot of the Cotswolds, Maxim and Tart Middleton lived—two bachelors in a little thatched cottage of their own. These brothers were short, squarely built, with dark swarthy faces and looked, as near as I can describe it, like a pair of onion men from Brittany. They were drainers, probably laying most of the tile drains in the clay land which skirted Carrant Brook and the little River Isbourne which went through their village. This is reputed to be the only river in the country which flows due north. No doubt you, like myself, have been in lots of churches said to be the second smallest in the country; these legends get handed down, but they are at least interesting.

Maxim and Tart used simple tools—a couple of spades, forks, a graft—long and tapered—for digging the last part of their trenches, and then they used a cleanser for creating a semi-circular bottom to the trench and bringing out the last of the mud or crumbs according to the state of the land. The rough agricultural pipes were laid with a pipe hook—a tool with a right angled bend of iron rod with a wooden handle or stale. Maxim was the craftsman and he judged the fall for his drain to run down by what he termed 'the scowl of brow'; it just meant that years of experience had taught him how to judge the lie of the land. Good drains have a long life and some of Maxim's and Tart's are running today as the rain beats against the window pane as I write.

Maxim was a terrific conversationalist. He would at times break into an almost Shakespearian vein on a variety of subjects. I first met him when he was draining Umberlands Length—a field with a slight fall towards our main road ditch. He passed the time of day with me and then said, 'You be Tom Archer's bwoy, beunt ya?' 'Yes, that's right. Do you know Dad?'

'I know him, I a done many a mile of draining for him afore thee was as big as a shirt button.'

Then Maxim started quoting from the Psalms and about Moses striking the rock and the water gushing forth. From here we touched on a few of the Proverbs and then he spoke about women being deceitful above all things and 'desperate wicked.'

As we spoke, a tall ungainly man in an old Army overcoat cycled along the main road and turned up towards our village; it was Bert Hemming, Maxim's only nephew, or nevvy, as he called him. Bert was an odd job man, did a bit of everything. Suddenly Maxim's tone changed from his Bible quotations to his candid opinion of nevvy Bert—'that disreputable wretch, a-fillin' his intestin's with those filthy ingredients.' He swore, he blasphemed and I heard Bert's character in no uncertain terms. 'The drunken hound, leading my sister the life he did until she died last year. Did you hear about him getting into bed with his breeches and boots and gaiters on, Master Archer?'

'No,' I said, 'but it was a bad thing to do to get between clean sheets like that.'

'Ah,' said Maxim, 'he'd been threshing at Wetherfields and come home as full as a blowed tick with cider.'

'Why doesn't he go and live with his sister now his mother's dead?' I asked.

'Oh the diabolical, vulgar beast,' Maxim said. 'Oi udn't trust him as far as I could spet, he ud like enough want to take a liberty with her when he'd had his fill of that awful liquor.'

At this moment Tart came down the field carrying the red clay drain pipes under each arm. Said Maxim, 'We beunt a goin' to leave our feow coppers to that waster, be us?'

Tart answered, 'Not likely after we have worked hard and then let him run it down the drain at some pub's urinal.'

Maxim had strong views on the Church and parsons in general and when the village parson and his wife left he told me, 'Thur was a tay party, some of the folks who think themselves above us were there and I a bin told as some of them women as a done nuthin' but run the parson's wife down, when it came to the time to say goodbye to her, kissed her—slobbering, I calls it, the great hypocrites,' then he quoted out of the 'word', as he called the Bible, about the Pharisee.

Tart said, 'We walked through the village a Sunday and they be building a bungalow anant the blacksmith's shop. Did ever you see such work? A poor paltry job I calls it. They a got them bricks with holes through um and the stritchers as goes through the nine-inch wall shows daylight right through. I reckons they ull get the rats and the mice in thur and possibly the rabbits.' The bungalow was cement rendered after filling up all the holes, but the Middletons still thought it a poor and paltry job. 'I a bin up in Ashton churchyard, Tart and me walked up thur last Sunday, there's a grave or two of some of our relatives.' Then Maxim, after placing another tile drain in the bottom of his trench, spitting on his hands to get a better grip of the pipe hook, said, 'I'll gu to Hanover if thur unt some dead folks up in Ashton churchyard. I a bin thinkin' they a bin buryin' thur this last eight hundred years and if they only buried ten a year, that's eight thousand of um. My eyes, that's a lot of dead folks—as many folks as there be livin' in Tewkesbury. Well, we shall have to get a move on, Tart, you knows what it says "slothfulness casteth into a deep sleep and an idle soul shall suffer hunger". Proverbs 19, verse 15.'

So I left the drainers. They, too, have gone now into the last deep sleep.

CHAPTER SIXTEEN

OUTRIGHTS

WHEN I was a boy, our old farm workers had an unusual name for people who come round the villages from the town shops, stores and warehouses taking orders for goods; they called them the 'Outrights'. Perhaps this was a variation on the word 'Outrider', but anyway they were travellers or 'representatives' as we would call them today.

Outrights came in devious ways. The majority cycled, some came by horse and trap, others by train and one or two had cars. Hubert from Tewkesbury was in the grocery trade; he cycled over every other Friday to get the order to be delivered by horse and van the next Tuesday. He travelled round most of the villages within eight or nine miles of Tewkesbury and somehow I think we were one of the outposts of his little empire. He was a tall, upright man, smartly dressed in Norfolk Jacket, breeches and stockings with boots well 'Cherry Blossomed'; military in bearing with a fierce-looking waxed moustache.

Hubert Outright, or Harding, had a good round in our village. He had become a household word; people seldom thought of giving him up, and he had served my grandfather and the Bradfields long before the '14 war. One of his best customers was Charlie Bradfield who had a large family; Hubert arrived there about teatime and Charlie, getting his spoke in first, started off:

'Now, Master Hubert, I a got a bone to pick along a you.'

'Have you, Charlie, now what's the trouble?'

'I'll be dalled if you didn't send us some cheese last fortnit—what did the Mussus order—five pounds, wasn't it?—and you sent us eight.'

'Sorry about that, Charlie.' Hubert looked really worried. 'It's the girls in the shop. It won't happen again and there's a pint of cider paid for you at the Plough.'

With this, when Charlie had finished tea, he left the ordering to Mrs. Bradfield and went to the Plough to make sure of his pint. It happened again but the pint was always up at the Plough for Charlie. Tom Wheatcroft described Hubert as 'a generous mon; he treated all as was in the Plough every other Friday night.'

It was about eight o'clock when he arrived at our house. He knocked loudly on our front knocker (he was deaf) and this started our two dogs barking. Dad took the candle to the door to let him into the hall, then into the oil-lit living room. If it was raining in the winter or a cold wind blowing, Dad bawled into his ear, 'What a terrible night.'

'Yes, yes, yes,' Hubert answered, 'not like I suffered on the Somme though.'

As he sat by our fireside with just enough cider in him to make him talkative, he related some of his experiences. I shoved my homework book on one side as Hubert said, 'I started soldiering in the Royal Horse Artillery before I went in the trenches.' He described in detail how he drove his gun carriage to the front, laid his gun, wheeled round as he rode the foremost horse, then back hell for leather. I saw the lot—the shells, the leather-covered traces of the horses, the hubs on the carriage wheels and Hubert in puttees, spurs and tunic, and learned how the noise of the guns made him deaf.

'Many rats about in the corn ricks, Mr. Archer?' he asked Dad.

'We don't grow any corn now, Hubert,' Dad again cupped his hand and hollered into Hubert's earhole.

'Ha, I suppose it's the foreign stuff being so cheap, but you boys' (he turned to me and my brother) 'have never seen rats.' Old Tiddles, our tabby cat, stretched herself on the rag rug in front of the oven grate.

'I've seen rats,' said Hubert (the cider was working), 'bigger than that cat in the trenches on the Somme.' We had rats in the outhouse where the fowl corn was kept and I had later on in the evening to go up there with a candle to fetch the fire-lighting wood for morning. If ever I see one tonight, I shall have a blue fit, I thought, and sometimes the wind blew the candle out and that meant finding my way back in the dark.

'Now, Mrs. Archer, your order,' Hubert said, undoing a piece of black garter elastic from around his little blue book. 'Flour, self-raising, currants, sugar...' he went through the lot. One week he said, 'Pepper,' and cupped his ear.

'No, not this week,' Mother said.

'Pepper's going up,' said Hubert. 'Just in confidence it's going to be dear. Some of the big businesses are cornering it, get plenty of pepper in now you have the chance.' Mother ordered a small quantity but I had visions of her ordering enough to fill a Huntley and Palmers biscuit tin—in fact, enough to last us about fifty years.

Now Hubert prided himself on their tea, 'specially blended for the waters of the district, your water's got a lot of lime in it, you know,' he said. 'I take so much Darjeeling, so much Ceylon and I mix these different types and you will agree that it is a blend second to none.'

For three fortnights Mother had not ordered tea and Hubert became suspicious. 'Anything wrong with our tea?' he queried. Mother had to admit that Dad, who was a martyr to indigestion, had fancied a brand reputed to prevent it. Hubert was not impressed. 'You won't beat mine, they can't blend tea to suit the waters of Bredon.' Another week Mother ordered sauce and forgot to state the size of the bottle, Hubert sent a café size! It stood on our breakfast table pointing to the ceiling like one of Hubert's guns. But Hubert was a good man to both his employers and his customers. I fancy if a family fell on hard times he would help to foot the bill, keeping them afloat until the tide turned. I don't expect he ever realised that he did a little to break the monotony of some people's winter evenings.

Bastin's were known in Evesham as shoe and boot makers. The trade in made-to-measure shoes and boots was almost dead when I was a boy but Bastin's still did some for old customers. They also repaired boots and shoes; the solers and heelers of shoes Dad always referred to as 'snobs'. Bastin's had their Outright who must have been one of the last of the packmen. He called at our house with his pack of boots for the farm workers, hobnailed, tea drinkers or light boots for Sunday, and brands known as Little Dukes and Little Gents for us boys. I felt no end of a fellow when I wore my first pair of Little Gents, laced, with holes half way, then hooks for the top two or three rows.

He also carried laces—cotton and leather—shoe polish and dubbin which was a very necessary part of a farm worker's gear. I have seen our cowman with a pair of Bastin's Plough and Harrow boots plastered in dubbin, stand in the horse trough with the water up to near the top of the lace holes. Leather was waterproof—it had to be, there were no rubber wellington boots. Bastin's Outright also took boots in for repair, but he was particular, the boots had to be their own brand. I well remember the smell of leather at the shop. The exciting smell of a pair of new boots. Wonders have been worked in plastics but the mellow look and feel of tanned hide is akin to beer aged in the wood. Farm workers anticipating winter's rough weather invested their harvest money in leather boots.

Bastin's had a stall in the Market Place at Evesham and it was an education to watch Mr. Bastin himself cutting leather laces with such precision out of a sheet of leather. The old market gardeners bought these.

One Outright I well remember, a Mr. Marks, who sold fertiliser. He came round in a two-seater car and dicky, was immaculately dressed in a light grey suit and had a carnation in his buttonhole. Dad bought 'artificial', as we called it, by the truck load—smelly Peruvian guano, meat and bone, fish manure, and Mr. Marks sold the lot. He, like Hubert, was deaf but he had a hearing aid; one wit said that you shouted in one ear for sulphate of ammonia and in the other for superphosphate. If Dad ordered three tons of artificial, Mr. Marks with his book out would say, 'Make it five tons, it comes cheaper,' and he would write down five. Sometimes Dad would say, 'All right then, but don't send it until I send you a postcard, the artificial house is almost full.'

What a senseless way they had of packing these fertilisers in those days—always in two-hundredweight bags which had to be hauled out of the railway vans, and oh, the smell of some of it! It was definitely not artificial to me. The meat and bone was coarse ground, with bits of cow horn clearly visible in the bags; the fish was beyond description. Mr. Marks sold nothing but the best and his breezy, cheerful personality inspired the growers in our vale. When prices in the market were good, the growers really ploughed back their profits into the ground. Mr. Marks was not a high-pressure salesman, but a good adviser of the best manure to use; he had to meet his customers again on market day.

CHAPTER SEVENTEEN

PEG LEG STUBBINS

IF EVER you climb the south side of Bredon Hill, what will strike you are the scattered little farmsteads, each with its barn and foldyard—stone built and stone slated. There is something Welshlike in their placing in little folds of the hill; Bredon, I believe, is derived from the Welsh. The names of these holdings gives a friendly, welcoming sound—Sundial Farm, La Loo, Sheldons, Cobblers, Paris, Shaw Green.

Peg Leg Stubbins lived in one of these outposts about seven hundred feet up looking towards the Cotswolds and a little of the Avon valley just before it joins the Severn at Tewkesbury. He had lost a leg serving with his County regiment in the Boer War and it would not have been an exaggeration to have called him 'Capability' after the great landscape gardener, or perhaps, better still 'Schemer' after Schemer Keyte from Broadway who invented the first sewing machine using an elm board as its base.

Peg Leg brought up his little family and earned his living as a stone-breaker, his wooden leg being no great handicap to him when he arrived at his work. After he had broken the largest of the Clee Hill stones with a sledge-hammer, he sat on the heap of stone by the road and used much smaller hammers for bringing them down to the right size for road making; it is a well known saying around these parts—'as hard as Clee Hill stone'. These stones from the border country with Wales are good material for roadmaking, they don't crush and go mushy like the softer Cotswold stone which forms Bredon Hill. Peg Leg's oval-shaped small hammers had nut sticks for helves or shafts; he cut these out of the coppice and the rhythm of his hammering and the springing of the nut sticks created an action not unlike that of a kettledrum player; you see, he got so many blows into a minute's work. He told me, 'Allus follow the vein of the stone, same as you would if you were breaking coal.' He wore the usual gauze spectacles to protect his eyes; it was fairly common in those days for a stone-breaker who failed to take this precaution to lose an eye. Peg Leg's ingenuity came out in his invention of a kind of tricycle to propel himself up and down the hill. The three-furrow, one horse drill has disappeared from the farming scene—I have one in the barn now, just a museum piece. Peg Leg's tricycle consisted of the bare frame of one of these drills (wooden) with wooden-spoked wheels with iron rims made at the blacksmiths out of half-inch round iron. In an artful way he converted the gearing which turned the cogs on the seed boxes so that two levers, also made of ash wood, could be pulled backwards and forwards and so propel the contraption along. He fixed the front wheel with an iron collar just where the horse would be hitched if it were a drill. This wheel could be turned for steering with a piece of rope. Stubbins sat amidships, his peg leg straight out along the framework. With this primitive invalid chair he travelled as far as Beckford railway station, a distance of four miles, and a raw young porter seeing him come down the road bridge said, 'Well I'll be dalled if I 'aint sin vehicles of all kinds come to this yer station, but never sin a mon a riding on a three-furrow wheat drill.'

CHAPTER EIGHTEEN

BUMPER MORGAN

HAVE YOU ever met a man who was so rural, such a student of nature, that to have placed him in a city street would have been like putting a carthorse in the paddock at Ascot? Bumper is such a man, a typical Uncle Silas. When he talks he half sits, half lies on his Victorian sofa. He is a big man, getting a bit rheumaticky, his arms smelling of menthol and wintergreen, but as he told me, 'The doctor says it don't matter what you rub on 'um at eighty-four, it won't cure it—ony ease it.'

I said, 'Well, I suppose we all have to expect something when we get older.'

'Oi, you a said it now,' he retorted, 'we gets it whether we expects it or no. Mind ya,' he went on, 'we beunt the nation 'a we was.'

'Why, then, Mr. Morgan?' I said.

'Well, let's consider a bit; you bin to the Grammar School and I left when I was eleven year old. All the cream a British manhood was killed in the '14 war, now we be breeding from the rejects—the rag tag and bobtail as survived.' He then went on to tell me tales of the Somme and how he was in the Terriers about 1910 at camp on Salisbury Plain.

'The old Kaiser came and all his Generals just to ferret out what he could find. Then mind ya, when I was called up old Kitchener didn't care for we, but I did see the young Prince of Wales at the front, a courageous young fella.'

Bumper lived in his stone cottage well up on our hill.

'Nice view,' I said.

'You might think so,' came back the reply as he pulled himself up on to the sofa and smoothed out his tobacco-stained moustache. 'There's a skinny wind a-blowin' straight from Russia.' He knew a bit of geography. 'There's nothin' between me and the Urals. Bist a comin' up into the shed? I a got summat to show ya.'

It was a sunny day, apart from the wind not bad for October.

We left the snugness of his living room where a fire roared halfway up the chimney of his old oven grate. 'Thee hast got a bit of a cold, ain't you?' he said to me. 'Now, I never gets one, allus eats plenty of raw onions. I like 'em boiled with butter on. Might have some tonight. The doctor told me this morning he had got a streamer and could do nothing about it.'

'Why ever didn't you tell him to have some onions, Bumper?' I said and he then went on to give his opinion of the medical profession. 'You see all they gives out today is pills. Pills for everything, a got about four different colours, but onions be the thing, come and have a look at mine hung up in the shed.' He gave me a few for boiling. 'Now what dust think of my taters?— Ayron summat they be. I just weighed some, almost two pound apiece.'

'What sort of artificial do you use, Mr. Morgan?'

'Don't thee get mentioning that tack to me, drawing all the nature out of the ground and taking all the flavour out of the vegetables. What I uses in pig muck. See that big yup at the top of my ground, that's all chock full of ammonia just now. Then there that yup of soot in the corner, I'm leavin' that to mella— new soot burns, yer see.'

Bumper had a few sows left but he went on to tell me that 'pigs be either muck or money and they be muck now. Twelve shillings a sixpence apiece for weaners in the market the last lot I took,' he said. 'Nobody can stomach that fur long, I be getting out of pigs except one for meself. But mind, taters growed with natural stuff a got the flavour and the experts says according to the paper as there ain't no analysis in soot but, my boy, ma taters digs as clean as a whistle. Mind when you be eighty-four you mistrusts Ministries and papers.'

Bumper got his name for his prowess as a fast bowler in village cricket. 'About fifty years ago,' he told me, 'I could send 'um down, mind. You won't remember that chap being killed a playin' for the next village?'

'No, that was a bit before my time.'

'Well,' Bumper went on, 'it was a hot summer, we don't get the summers like it now, nor the day 'unt so long. I a bin haymaking many a time at half past ten a night. Still, what was I a sayin'? Oh cricket ... the next Saturday after that young

chap was killed we was a playin' the Cheltenham Plece [police].
Our ground was devilish hard and cracked, Percy, our wicket-
keeper captain, put me on to bowl. The first ball I was a bit
wide of the tack and the second I dropped him just a bit short
into a bit of plantain, up cocked the ball fastish and ketched this
policeman right in the jowl.'

'The jowl?' I said; we were back talking pig language.

'Thee knows't where I means—by the Adam's apple. Down he
went.' Mr. Bumper Morgan smacked his lips and tapped his pig
bench in the shed with the blade of a breast plough he picked
up on the floor. 'Down he went,' he repeated, 'just like a stone.
He showed the whites of his eyes smartish and they carried him
off. The next bloke to come in was a sergeant—a big, tall fella.
Do you know I dropped the next ball straight in the same place
on that plantain and he come up about the same. This yer
sergeant ducked, ya see, to let the ball go over his head, but he
was unlucky. The seam of the ball skimmed his one eyebrow
and took a layer or two of skin with it.'

' "Three to come," said Percy, "and we don't want a repeti-
tion of last week, send 'em down very steady and that'll do with
your bowling for today." '

We sat on the pig bench and all around were his 'whim
whams' as he called them—bird traps, muzzle-loaders, black
powder, rabbit net, wires, traps, his channilor for planting his
peas and beans, rakes made by himself with six-inch nails for
the teeth, a little barrel of rhubarb wine and another of parsnip.
Back in the house he told me of Sunday nights long ago when
he biked forty-odd miles from by Bristol from his brother's
place, along what is now the A38, and never met a vehicle of any
sort until he got to Tewkesbury. 'Them was carbide lamps we
used, and you can guess what we did when the water ran dry in
the top. When we went on the village roads, the only place to
ride was in the wheel ruts. Did you ever see a cushion-tyred
bike?' he said.

I had seen one in a museum, I told him. Bumper said it
wasn't much of a ride. 'Still,' he said, 'the spring carts worn't
exactly Riles Rices.' Bumper's remarks about what we are breeding from made me think that if he'd married his stock might
have approached the kind that were lost in 1914 to 1918.

CHAPTER NINETEEN

JIM AND THE COMPANY

'HE'S GOT a good job,' young Tom Wheatcroft said of his brother. 'He's on for the Company.' Most Ashtonians called the Midland Railway 'The Company'. Jim's a big chap, a willing chap, who worked on our farm, under-cowman to George Bendall. Part of his job was to take the seventeen-gallon churns of milk down to our station on the branch line at eight-ten a.m. This line went as far as Ashchurch, joining the Birmingham–Bristol main line. The milk was transferred to the main line train for Birmingham at Ashchurch.

Jim either used one of the cobs, Min or Tom in the milk float or else he took Flower in the dray, standing up like a man amidst the churns on the dray or sitting on the box seat at the back of the float. Our porter-in-charge (we couldn't run to a gold braided 'Station Boss', as they were known in the village) was not an easy man for boy-chaps to please. He was a sandy moustached, lean fellow who worked in the station in shifts with an under-porter. He was the sort of man who had two natures—his booking office manner when he issued tickets to all stations to Birmingham, or Ashchurch, could be quite charming, especially to the few first-class passengers who travelled on the line. But out in the siding when a truck of 'artificial' came in or when he was helping load sprouts, apples and all the riches of our village for the industrial north, we will say he was 'unco-operative'. Jim found this out when he first started taking our milk to the station. Seventeen gallons of milk plus the churn weighs something approaching two hundredweight and Jim was, like David of old, a stripling. The eight-ten to Ashchurch left platform 2 on the other side of the line. Jim usually arrived in good time and pulled the little four-wheeled trolley with Midland Railway painted alongside close up to his dray or float and waited for Wilf the porter-in-charge to come out of the station house and help him to load four or five churns on to the railway trolley in readiness to pull it across the level crossing and, with an extra push up, on to the opposite platform. Just as the front of the little tank engine, pulling about four coaches, emerged from underneath the road bridge. Wilf shot through the little white garden gate and made for Jim. The churns were manoeuvred with difficulty on to the trolley, Jim doing his best and Wilf swearing his best. Meanwhile the guard was getting impatient and the engine driver had to reverse the train to enable Wilf and Jim to cross the level crossing with their load. This thing happened most mornings and young Jim's elder brother told him, 'If old Wilf keeps on swearing at you, ask him for a paper or form so that you can report him to Derby.'

Next morning Wilf gave Jim his usual mouthful and, although a little nervous, Jim plucked up courage and said to Wilf: 'I've had enough of your language every morning. Give me a form to fill in and I'll report ya to Derby.' Wilf ran into the booking hall followed by Jim, Wilf's moustache bristling as he used every swear word and oath he knew and some that Jim had not heard before. In a mad passion, he opened one drawer after the other, throwing forms in all directions.

'Report me to Derby, you little snot, I'll report you to your gaffers.'

'Oh, Wilf,' said Jim, 'Bendall wants another consignment book.' This upset him still more. 'You chaps uses our consignment books for toilet paper, you only had one the other day.'

Jim had many more battles with Wilf but never again did he threaten to report him to Derby.

Cold winter evenings when Jim had sprouts to load for all points north, Wilf took a lot of coaxing out of his snug booking office. 'Go and get the truck lid down, it's the fifth one along for Nottingham, I'll be along in a minute.' Young Jim had often unloaded his half ton and struggled to fasten the truck lid before Wilf ambled along the siding, blowing his hands and with half a Woodbine hanging from under his moustache. 'Some empty churns on the platform,' Wilf would say and he did help young Jim on to the dray with them. Sometimes a churn of milk came back sour; we had to pay the carriage on it and Wilf's pig, which he kept in an old railway carriage under the pear tree, had sour milk with his barley meal for a few days. At the other end, George Bendall was worried about Jim catching the milk train and also that he had plenty of empty churns for the milk; perhaps three or four cows calved in a week and up went the gallonage of milk. One morning George came to our back door and said to Dad, 'Dalled if I knows what to do with the milk, we got no churns.' Jim took him up into the long shed to dig a hole and put it in, but old George said, 'Thee talks like one of they foolish women, I wish thee udns't talk so, jumping stupid amongst all this work.' Then the kicking cow calved and Jim had to hold her by the nostrils while old George milked her—a tiresome job.

You will have gathered that besides being under-cowman, Jim was dray man as well. He made journey after journey to the station with fruit and vegetables and brought back artificial manure, cattle cake in huge flat slabs, cotton cake and linseed cake from Gloucester to be unloaded at our station. 'Demurrage' was a word we got used to early in life—it just meant that if a truckload of goods was not emptied within a certain time Demurrage money was due to pay the Company.

When Jim loaded produce on the Great Western he had to take Flower and the dray six miles each way to Evesham. This only occurred when we loaded for Cardiff. Dad put thirty bags of sprouts on Jim's dray for Cardiff, and at Evesham G.W.R. station the porter and Jim could only make it twenty-nine. A pouring wet November day is not the best time to ride on a horse dray. Jim sat on one bag of sprouts covered with a few old sacks just to keep his latter end drier and more comfortable than it would have been on the boarded bed of the dray. Returning into the yard that night Dad said, 'What's that you are sitting on, Jim?' Of course it was the missing bag of sprouts which had made the return trip from Evesham.

No trains ran on our branch line on Sundays, so Jim took our milk seven miles Sunday mornings to catch the main line train to Birmingham at Ashchurch station. On those early Sunday mornings in the twenties, drays, spring carts and floats travelled the roads leading to Ashchurch station. It is a fact that horses enjoy racing one another whether it's at point-to-point meetings, hunting, or just nags, cobs and ponies drawing their loads to the railway station. Jim met many of his friends along the Tewkesbury–Stow road those Sunday mornings. Flower, in our dray, could hold her own against horses driven by other farm lads and Jim has told me how he gave her that extra bit of corn in the week and saw to it she was well shod, and in his words 'her showed um the way to Ashchurch'.

Flower was an ideal dray horse—deep and broad shoulders and nimble feet—but according to Walt the carter and the other men, young Jim spoilt her in one way. Jim, with the leather reins in one hand, would click his tongue as he walked by her near flank and at the same time drop the reins just gently down on her back. This was the signal—Flower started off at the trot and Jim, lissom and agile, sprang seat first on to the front corner of the dray as it passed. Now the older men disagreed with this, always reckoning to be comfortably seated before the horse moved off. When they took Flower anywhere, she behaved as she did with Jim and old men got angry sometimes and young Jim got the blame. As Flower got older she, of course, got a bit slower. There were alternative horses for the dray but Jim viewed them with very little enthusiasm. 'Boxer,' he said, 'be all right if you got all day,' and Tom, the nag, was old and frightened of motor-bikes. Down in Didcot Ham, Walt turned up some of the younger horses; Violet, a black mare, one he called Slarrops—Walt said he had got 'humour in his fit', I suppose it was grease—then there was a nice bay mare, out of a thoroughbred by a shire stallion, named Pleasant. Pleasant had 'stole the oss' in the Captain's Hill on Bredon and produced a nice colt buckshee, as Walt said. When her colt was weaned, Pleasant had only been broken in to trace work, or working in chains. One March morning, most of the horses were working and young Jim had to fetch a load of gillies (wallflowers) out of Clay Furlong and take them to the station for Manchester. Pleasant had never been in shafts and against all the advice of his elders, Jim put Pleasant in the dray. I can see him now as he trotted her gently along the Grafton footpath, Jim standing upright on the front of the dray. 'Mind what thee bist at,' said Walt. 'Once they runs away it becomes a habit, they be allus at it.'

George Bendall said. 'What bist a goin' to do if a train lets off steam at the station?' But Jim said Pleasant had been in Didcot Ham and was used to the sound of trains. Neither Jim, Pleasant, nor the gillies came to any harm. He loaded them with the Company and from that day Pleasant showed her paces along the roads to market and station.

Jim said to me, 'Her had to go in shafts some day.'

CHAPTER TWENTY

ADSCRIPTUS GLAEBAE
(CLOSE TO THE SOIL)

THE YOUNG Squire, Humphrey, and his friend Roland were what was known as landed gentry, but their position and their ample money kept them aloof from such things as the state of the soil, the weather and, to a great extent, farm prices.

Frank Wheatcroft told me, 'You know as I unt one to pry into other folks' business, but make no mistake them two gentlemen a got a smart bit a money salted down. I beun't one as understands the stock market—the only market I ever gus to is A'sum cattle fair on Candlemas if our gaffer is buying a good oss.'

'No, Frank,' says I. 'You keeps yourself very much to yourself.'

'I keeps to my station,' he said. 'If we don't get some frost this spring, planting ull be devilish bad, but that yunt my worry.'

He emptied his glass of rhubarb wine and turned his thoughts to the past.

'You know where old Roland lives by the sycamore tree?' he said.

'Course I do. I only spoke to him yesterday.'

'Well, as I told ya afore,' said Frank, 'Roland was a bit ronk when he was younger.'

'You mean rank?'

'Oi, that be it; what I myuns is that he very soon got a bit fresh with any fine ooman.'

'I understand,' I said.

'You knows that thatched house by the Cross? Well, thur used to be two houses thur, not one. Long afore thy time, thee Dad ud remember,' he continued. 'In the corner house thur was a mon as wasn't one for work, you understands my meaning?' There were about four of us listening to his story. 'Now I don't want any on ya to think I be talking nast or filth, we be all growed up and married and understands these things.'

'What was unusual, Frank?' I butted in.

'I be just a comin' to that. Her used to get the livin'. Oi, her was a most beautiful ooman, a fine figure—well made. Her hair was a kind of bluey black like them jackdaws as nests in the gargoyles of the church. Up yur'—and he held his braces away from the flannel shirt covering his broad chest—'her had got a pair,' and we detected a twinkle in his eye as he moistened his mouth with his tongue, making no secret of the fact that he would have liked to have courted, or kept company, with her. With a quick turn towards me he said, 'You understands what I myuns when I tells ya that Roland cohabited with her regular? Mind, he wasn't the only one by any manner or means. Humphrey, who was always a bit foolhardy, got Charlie Bradfield to play um a trick. Humphrey had bin threshing a few oats for his hunters and Charlie had put the chaff in the tub in the nag stable. He told Charlie to get a sheet full of chaff on a bright moonlight night just after Christmas and lay a trail of this 'ere chaff from Roland's front gate to this ooman's gate.'

Frank went rambling on as the glasses of rhubarb wine loosened his tongue and told what he described as 'the sartin' truth'. 'I was one as saw this trail of chaff the following morning. Mind, it never stopped Roland. Her was a beautiful ooman, I wish I could remember her name. It'll no doubt come to me when you be gone.' With another swig of rhubarb wine he said, 'The best of health.'

t. Barbara's Church and moat pond, Ashton-under Hill, before 1913

Bill Spires holding a twenty-one hundredweight bull

The Sprout Picking Championship

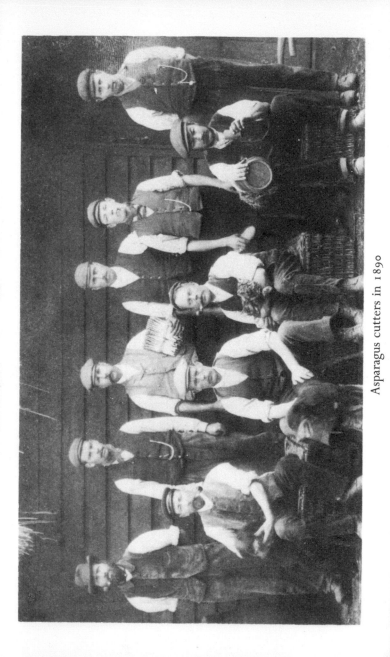

Asparagus cutters in 1890

Asparagus tiers in 1890

On a farm at Grafton early this century

Cutting pit props on Bredon Hill

Badgers and dog ready for baiting on Cotswold's Edge

CHAPTER TWENTY-ONE

BACHELORS' AVENUE

THE NARROW winding lane, steeply banked on either side, had at the bottom end a row of thatched black and white cottages, then further up the slope were the odd farm house of stone, the Georgian brick and a Victorian three-storeyed house which would have looked more in place as the home of a country town merchant. So many of the people up there were unmarried that it got the unofficial name of Bachelors' Avenue. In the Victorian house lived Edward Stidiford, artist and musician, who pottered about his orchard and for some unknown reason was generally known as Tiddley. Many is the hour I have spent with Tiddley sitting in the summer-time on the wooden seat in his front garden. Outside his gate ran one of the many streams of spring water off the hill and the footpath had lots of little stone bridges crossing the stream. The old folk called it the Causeway; Charlie Bradfield spoke of 'walking down the Cause'.

I suppose it is difficult for a man to live alone for seventy-odd years in a village without being considered a little eccentric. I would rather describe Tiddley as interesting. We hear a lot about natural gardens and nature reserves and Tiddley's garden and orchard was just that. He did mow what he called 'the heth' off the thistles and nettles once a year with his scythe, but in the main the birds and the rabbits took over and the ivy and brambles entwined themselves around the moss covered tree trunks. The apple trees were nondescript but some of the fruit had a subtle flavour. He gave it to all and sundry and the flavour of his mellow burgundy pears lingers with me still. If Tiddley had marketed his Nine Square apples or his Russets, I doubt if they would have paid for the picking; he did make a drop of good cider for his older friends, but I was just a boy.

In Tiddley's house his studio with its bay window overlooked the wilderness of his orchard. His pictures of landscapes in oil were considered good by the people who knew and he had some hung in art exhibitions and the second-class galleries. One I remember was of an old apple tree which had fallen over in his orchard, taken root again, and from its horizontal trunk it grew fifteen feet vertically and formed a shapely head. He painted it in full bloom with its moss covered bark. This particular year Tom Bosworth had put a bunch of ewes and lambs in the orchard to take advantage of a bit of early keep and Tiddley painted a fine water colour of the little scene with the Oxford ewe licking her two young lambs under the beautifully natural old tree. Tom told me in confidence, 'I takes my yows and lambs out into my own orchards nights, you see there's so much that they can get tangled up in in Tiddley's. I dare say the foxes comes down off the Nap a rabbiting, there's plenty of cover.'

I spoke of Tiddley as a musician. He had a violin which he told me was a Strad; it certainly was a fine instrument and he played me some beautiful pieces on those summer nights when the wireless was still only paper talk. 'Shall we try The air on the G String?' he asked me one evening. This gave me an appetite for more and he had learnt by practice to imitate the sound of the wind on that old violin of his, but we didn't sit on that seat for too long before he asked me into his cool stone-slabbed dining room. In the window was a long mahogany table which was covered with rose petals and the perfume in that room was heavenly. The petals were drying up and I was curious. 'Why all those petals on the table?' I asked.

'Oh, tobacco, my boy, is taxed more and more every year. I grow my own, come and see.'

There, on the sunny side of the garden, was one crop tended with care, growing huge leaves of the nicotine plant also ready for drying in his shed. 'You see, my boy, I mix the home grown tobacco with the rose petals and make my smoking mixture.' He lit his pipe and I must say the aroma was pleasing and it must have satisfied him too.

Tiddley's clothes were well worn and threadbare; he kept himself clean but would allow no woman in his house. He was educated at a famous Public School which he told me played cricket with the Fosters who caused Worcestershire County Cricket Club to be known as Fostershire. He spoke of Grace and the great men.

How sad it is when a man like Mr. Stidiford becomes infirm!

As a boy I knew he kept himself and his house spick and span, although he chose to let his garden and orchard remain wild. Old age plays funny tricks and it is far more evident in the country where most things that go on are common knowledge. Tiddley let himself go as we say; first he was not so clean as he had been, his roof leaked, he couldn't mow the heth of the natural plant life in his garden and he didn't seem to care. I had mixed feelings when I visited him towards the end. My first thoughts were what good a woman could have done in that household of his at this stage. He had what he described as a snivelling cold and he was sitting by the fire hotting up some of his cider in a saucepan; this he was taking with rosemary to cure his cold. I went up into his bedroom, it was cold, damp and draughty. He had left the sash window open so long that a branch of one of his apple trees had grown right into the room and there by his bed were the signs of how he knocked his pipe out on the apple branch before he retired. 'I'll bring the saw up and saw off that branch for you,' I told him.

'No, my boy, it's company that branch on windy nights and as you see I knock my pipe out on it.'

'I'm sorry to see you not so well, Mr. Stidiford, shall I call the doctor?'

'No, no, don't do that,' he said. 'He will have me in hospital and this place will get cold and damp, I just couldn't see it getting like that. I tell you,' he said, 'I'm too miserable to live and too wicked to die.'

'Don't say that, Mr. Stidiford. You have at least taught me lots of things about life in general. You'll pick up; can I get you anything?'

'No,' said Tiddley. 'Come with me into the back place,' and there were a heap of tins on the floor as big as a potato bury.

'Why don't you get the Council to take your refuse?' I said. 'You pay your rates.' But senility had made him loathe to throw anything away. The bureau bookcase in his studio had a broken pane. 'I'll tell you the history of that,' he said. 'Millie Bosworth was governess to me before I went away to school; one day she boxed my ears and I threw the pencil box at her and she ducked and hence the broken bookcase; it was never mended.' Tiddley religiously observed one day during the year. Why, I don't know. It was the Fifth of November. On the night of the Fifth, Tiddley loaded his muzzle-loader gun and shot up into his apple trees to the delight of boys who couldn't afford fireworks. He loaded and reloaded all the evening, the black powder forming a pall of smoke in his little orchard. 'Here,' he said to me on my last visit, 'take this gun just to remember me by.' The doctor came and he died in hospital soon after. No, I don't think his was a wasted life. I have two of his pictures in oils and I still hear The air on the G String when I pass that old orchard.

Elijah Bendall, or Lijah, lived in the Avenue—one of the few who weren't bachelors. He lived next door to Cyril Gardner, a confirmed bachelor. Cyril's boss was a man with a keen sense of humour. When he was strawberry hoeing up in the Ten Acre Piece, Cyril cut a plant up with his hoe and made a hole to bury it so that the boss wouldn't see it. But the boss was sitting on his shooting stick further down the field just watching the men working.

'Am I going to have an invitation to the funeral?' he asked Cyril.

'What funeral, gaffer?' asked Cyril.

'Well,' the boss said, 'you have just buried a strawberry plant,' and they all had a good laugh.

In passing, I remember hoeing sprouts one day and remarking that I hadn't cut a plant up all day. Tom Wheatcroft said, 'Oh, then you beunt a getting close enough to the plants then.'

But Cyril's neighbour Lijah was a different card trump—rosy cheeked, side whiskers, short and stocky, a carter, all his life spent with horses. Tom Wheatcroft called him a passionate man and as I grew from boyhood to hobblehoy and then to manhood, I discovered that there were various sorts of passion and that the only one worth while was the feeling that a young man had for a young girl. Lijah's passion was different—it was temper. Ploughboys told me how they had been afraid of him when he threw clats of clay at them and the horses when things went wrong. I once saw him crying in temper by the side of a reaping machine because the job went bad. He beat the horses so that when he entered the stable they would get up in the manger and back away from him. A friend of mine who drove his horses at the plough saw him one morning hit his knuckles against the stable door post and knock the skin off. At times he was quiet and sensible and spoke kindly to the horses, but the slightest upset and he would attack the plough with a seven-pound felling axe. He was not really a suitable man to be with animals although he fed and looked after them well.

He was binding or reaping corn in Cinder Meadow when, as he said, it went devilish bad. Stan, the boy with the horses, couldn't do anything right and one adjustment after another just wouldn't get the machine in shape for cutting and tying the corn. The summer of 1921 it was, one of the hottest and driest summers in living memory. Lijah took the plough spanner, a heavy tool with a hammer head at one end, and struck the main driving cog a mighty swipe, knocking the cast-iron cog into scores of pieces. The land was cracked or chauned at the time following the drought; you could push a walking stick down these chauns. The pieces of the driving cog fell down these chauns and Lijah, afraid of what he had done in passion, got on his hands and knees too late to save the pieces. 'Stan,' he said, 'they be just got down to Australia.' The foreman arrived, summed up the situation and told Lijah to hook his horses off the Binder, put them on a heavy Larkworthy scuffle and scuffle a field adjoining. A fallow field with clats of earth as big as the wheels on the scuffle and a bad field for both carter and boy to walk over on a hot dusty summer's day. When I hear the word passion, I think of poor old Lijah. Mind you, constant soaking with rough cider didn't help his temper. It is a well-known fact in our village under the hill that he drank three hogsheads of cider himself one year.

David Dum was a small farmer, and despite the Vicar's words to him that it's not good for a man to live alone, he remained single. Besides his farm, he did hauling for the Council—stone off Holcomb Nap for the roads. He kept ten heavy Shire horses and before the new line was made from Honeybourne junction to Cheltenham, David hauled all the necessities of life with his heavy drays from Beckford station on our branch line to points way up on the Cotswolds. Walt was his head carter for some years. They started early in the morning with a horse and dray, and if the road to travel was a hilly one, they took a trace horse besides. Walt said to me quite recently:

'My boy, that was a job, getting ten osses in at five in the morning. I had to catch um all, mind, by Shaw Green, halfway up the hill, then tail um together tandem fashion an bring um down to Bachelors' Avenue and into the stable. Then mind,' he continued, 'I had to fill their nosebags with fittle corn chaff and hang these on the back axle of the drays. Ten o'clock some nights when the last dray came whome. I udn't do it agin mind, better to be in quod.' Walt described David as the biggest hypocrite that ever lived. 'Chapel bloke,' he added. 'No Saturday arternoons off and fifteen bob a week.' When I knew David he had mellowed with age. He still used two strawberry roan Shires to pull the water carts when our road was done in the macadam style.

The Primrose and the Violet Coppice were a part of David's estate. Here lay a part of David's wealth, for the whole area—a boggy hollow at one end and a mossy bank at the other—grew timber. No, it would be misleading to call it timber, it was a withy bed, or a sally bed, in the moister parts and an ash coppice on the drier bank.

The withies grew on stools or short stumps and were cut as osiers—bundles like boltings of straw—and sold to the Evesham hamper makers to make containers for market produce. Withies, gleaming and golden, were to be seen standing in their tidy bundles in the stream which skirted the coppice and flowed down the Avenue. This was to prevent them from drying out and keep them supple. The smaller osiers tied up the bundles of 120 buds of asparagus and the dozen bunches of spring onions ready for the market.

The sally or sallow stools grew poles suitable for ladder rungs. In the early spring, David's sally was a pleasing sight as the pussy willow buds changed colour almost daily. First a greenish grey and finally, as the buds turned to full bloom, the lemon yellow of the pollen became alive with bees. On these days in the spring of the year, David's sally was one of the first working places for the bees, the little wild bumble bees in particular.

Master Dum, as some of my friends referred to David, had several hilly pastures for his horses. The Leasows, the Langet, Heets Hill, Canks Bank. 'Thistles,' Walt said. 'We wants a feow donkeys up there to ut um off.'

On the more level parts of the hill, Walt did a bit of thistle dinking in his spare time. Now thistle dinking is a way of describing taking two horses and an old mowing machine and cutting the heth (height) off the thistles. 'Some of them Scotch men [boar thistles], I could tie me osses up to un at bait time. I'll tell tha I have had a poser up there. Them banks, if you beunt very careful, ud soon have me and the machine ass over yud.' Walt was excused from cutting all the thistles and their seeds gave the finches a feast in the autumn. David also left a few fuzz or gorse bushes about on the hilly pastures.

Poachers are well known to carry long nets which they lay at night to catch rabbits and partridges. One thing which deters them are fuzz bushes and boar thistles; the nets get tangled in these and the driven rabbits or the squat partridges escape underneath them. David had to contend with poachers when the Dutch barns were built in our village and townees lodged in the labourers' cottages. Another batch of poachers were the gang who came to relay our branch railway. With ten horses to winter, David was obliged to make hay. He had two flat fields, the top one was a permanent ley and the other was mostly sainfoin—clover common in the Cotswolds. He also planted mangolds for his horses and sometimes a patch of oats.

Tom Wheatcroft said to me that 'honesty is the best policy, but it keeps you very poor'. Not all David's draymen were honest men, nor did they believe that rabbits—just a part of the great creation—were not common property. I somehow think that the Game Laws of the last century bred poachers galore. You can lead a country labourer but he won't be driven.

On dry, mildish autumn evenings, when folk start saying 'Don't the days draw in', David would be picking a few apples in the home orchard to store for the winter. Walt and the draymen had pulled the mangolds and put them into bury. Snatcher and Cocky, two of the draymen, had long nets and had netted rabbits on Bredon for years. Up on the level sainfoin hill, the rabbits made the ground seem almost alive at the edge of night; Snatcher had been helping David get his apples picked after tea and as he stood on the top round but one of a forty-round ladder, his eyes wandered towards the sainfoin field, level and green, just right for netting. The rabbits played and scuttled about, some about three parts grown. 'Tomorrow night, Cocky,' he said next morning as they hitched their horses in the drays, 'we'll get a few of them out. Rabbits be about eighteen pence a couple.'

Cocky said, 'Thee help old David a' apple picking after tea and I'll get things ready.'

The evening was fine with a nice breeze blowing from the firs—a south-westerly. Cocky went up the hill an hour before dusk and with a wheelbarrow bowled barrow load after barrow load of mangolds from the bury dropping them in a straight line across the sainfoin field. 'That ul 'tice um,' he thought, 'we'll leave it latish tonight.'

At eleven o'clock on that autumn night, he met Snatcher with his whippet dog and long net. They approached the field, the wind blowing in their faces, and were quiet as mice. Sure enough, the rabbits had found the mangolds and were lined up like a bunch of ewes at the trough. Snatcher carefully and quietly unrolled his long net, put his nut sticks in position so that it made a netting fence about two feet high the whole length of the sainfoin field. Cocky walked in a big enough arc to get behind the rabbits without disturbing them, then approached the field and walked along the line of mangolds. The rabbits ran towards Snatcher's nets and needless to say, Snatcher and his dog, working silently, caught the rabbits as they hit the net and bagged seventy-four. After paunching, the rabbits were hung in Cocky's wash-house overnight and put on the carrier's cart for Evesham the next day. That is to say, all but a few which Snatcher held back to supply his cronies in the pub the next night.

Did you ever see a poacher's pocket? I had one once in a Derby Tweed when I drove plough. It is surprising what they will hold; the pocket inside the jacket takes up all the lining both sides and right around the back. As Snatcher sipped his cider, the next night in the pub, his pocket was loaded with rabbits. The publican's dog and old Oliver's dog, Rough, got the wind of these rabbits and gave Snatcher no rest until he had distributed the poor man's dinner to his mates. I doubt if Old David missed the rabbits; there were plenty on his neighbour's land. Tom Wheatcroft said that David wasn't like the rest on us, he hadn't got a wife and hungry youngsters to feed.

Old David's dead now, the last of a long line of yeoman farmers. He wasn't a bad sort really but these old horsey types did appear to treat their horses rather better than their men. Snatcher's language was aptly described by David when he said, 'To talk to Snatcher is like putting a match to a powder magazine.' You see, he stuttered when agitated and used lots of four-letter words.

CHAPTER TWENTY-TWO

THE HARBOURMASTER

BILL CHARLTON came to our village from that legendary place known in the Vale as Appleton Docks. Bill was called the Harbourmaster, although the docks were just a landing stage on the Avon where barges tied up years ago. The oak bark, stripped from the fallen trees in our big wood, was loaded on the longboats, there to journey to Tewkesbury and the Severn and then on the canals to Birmingham. This oak bark was in demand by the tanneries for tanning the hides into leather. When Dad was in his teens, he spent one summer working with special gauges, stripping the bark off the trunks and the big limbs of the Ashton oaks. Bill Charlton was at Appleton Docks then and supervised the loading of the barges from the farm waggons. Frank Wheatcroft said, 'If thee wants to see a sight for sore eyes, then go to Appleton Docks about four o'clock one afternoon and see the pigeons milked; they sends it away in churns from thur to Brummigen for making cheese.'

I have known Frank a very long time and had been taken in by his legpulls before. 'Another thing they unloads off them barges moonlight nights is hurdle seed.'

'Oh yes,' I said, 'I suppose our hurdle maker who works opposite the sundial plants this in his garden. Pull the other leg, Frank!'

'I helped your brother Tom to take a load of withies to be made into hurdles for our shepherd only yesterday. He splits them with a cleaver. Hast watched him and did'st notice which end of the pole he started to split first?'

'Does it matter, Frank?' I said warily, having to admit that this was one thing which I thought unimportant.

'Matter,' said Frank, 'I'd say it do, you starts the little end of a pole, I'd thought for a moment I was talking to a growed up and not a hobblehoy,' he said as he spat on the ground, 'and I was going to tell tha which end of a ooman, but thee knowst enough already!'

'What else do they handle at the docks?' I asked.

'Well,' Frank continued, 'I have seen some little loads and some big uns.'

'Tell me about the big ones. I'll bet old Bill Charlton got excited about them.'

'He did an' all and as he 'as come to the little farm at the Wren's Nest, why don't you go and ask him.'

The following Sunday afternoon, my pal Geoff and I went down past the blacksmith's to the Wren's Nest. 'Mr. Charlton, I'd be glad to hear of some of the big loads you've unloaded at Appleton Docks,' I said seriously.

'I'd be glad to tell you, Fred. The biggest arrived just before I left the job—a devilish big load it was too.'

'On a longboat?' I enquired.

'Yes,' he said, and then went on to tell me. 'It was a specially big load—a ton of blowed up pig's bladders!' I had asked for it and Bill Charlton had proved true to form. Pigeons milk, hurdle seed and blowed up pigs' bladders—that was about enough from the Harbourmaster and Frank to last a bit.

Bill was now settled in the Wren's Nest and with a hard-working wife who made butter and kept a few fowls, he farmed in some sort of fashion. But Bill was not cast in the same mould as most of us, it was as if the clock had been put back fifty years. One morning I met him in the Blacksmith's Lane looking under the weather. You see, he never signed the pledge or wore a blue ribbon signifying that he was a total abstainer—it would have been just deceitful. He was very fond of a social glass but unfortunately it didn't stop there. 'You don't look very well this morning, Bill,' I said.

'No, my boy,' came the reply. 'I goes to the expense of it.'

On market days the boy who worked for him on the little farm, young Spud Price, sat up with Bill's wife in the farm kitchen waiting for an unsteady, merry, market-hearted Bill Charlton to arrive home. Spud put the pony in the stable on these occasions and helped Bill to undress and make his ungainly way up the narrow winding staircase of the Wren's Nest farm. Candlemas Fair, an important event in the farming calendar, Bill took his wife, Emma, with him, Emma doing a bit of shopping in town while Bill took his weaner pigs to the market pens and spent the rest of the day propping the bar up at the King's Head. Spud milked and fed the cows, had his tea and sat with only the cat for company by the kitchen fire. The old grandfather clock in the hall struck eight, then nine and when ten o'clock came, Spud got anxious. Then into the yard trotted the old pony, the candle lamps glimmering in the February darkness. Bill put one foot on the trap step as Spud steadied him down. 'Where is the Mistress?' asked Spud.

'Why, dall it if I 'aven't left her in A'sum!' Bill managed to mutter, bleary eyed and heavy breathed.

Spud got Bill in the kitchen and went back into town to find Emma; he met her after she had walked halfway home, laden with shopping.

Bill changed his pony or nag quite often. Spud described one as being particularly prompt or lissom, with a bit of the devil in her as she showed the whites of her eyes. Her name was Sharper.

Markets were held monthly in our next village, Bill and Sharper coming home late as usual. The night was beautiful with a bright moon, and Sharper was stepping smartly along the Rabbit Lane towards the allotments. Harry Potts, one of the allotment holders, had a patch of Telegraph peas just coming through the ground and had made a mankin [scarecrow], clothed it in some of his wife's cast-off garments and set it up by the hedge on the pea patch. The one arm, made from a hedge stake, pointed to the sky and suspended from it were tin cans with stones in them; the rattle of these scared the birds off Harry's peas. Sharper laid her ears as she saw this strange object over the hedge and as the cans rattled, she shied on to the grass verge. Then she bolted, breaking both shafts of Bill's trap, and ran hell for leather up the Church Way. Bill, a very dazed Bill, sat in his trap on the grass verge. When Spud came and found him, Bill told Spud something very comical had happened. 'I have either found a trap or lost a horse,' he said.

As the Harbourmaster got old and gouty, Spud did most of the work on the little holding known as the Wren's Nest. One monthly market day, Bill bought a belly of pigs—ten of them, and Spud remarked that they looked scruffy, their coats rough and unhealthy.

'They will be all right,' Bill said, 'with some skim milk and barley meal.'

But they weren't, they had swine fever, and Bill killed them and then buried them in quick lime.

'Spud,' he said, 'now for a drop of cider.' And sitting in the kitchen overlooking the rickyard where the pigs had been buried, Spud and Bill drank their cider and ate their bread and cheese.

'Am I seeing things?' Bill nudged Spud and almost made him swallow the lump of hard cheese.

'What the Hanover!' said Spud, and there in the rickyard a pig had resurrected from the grave and was running around the yard plasted in lime and blood. 'The gun, Spud, quick!' shouted Bill and in a flash Spud put the pig out of its misery; that was a near thing, they both agreed. They also agreed that if the copper had come by they would have been down at Gloster jail. Rough cider, metheglin, parsnip and rhubarb wine taken in large quantities play peculiar tricks with the mind. Bill had built up such a concentration of these potent drinks that he had turns of the blue devils. He would invite his neighbours in of an evening when these bouts took place and as they sat round the fire, Bill, in his chimney corner, saw the little people on the hob opposite the oven on his fireplace. 'There they dance,' he said, 'and there they pitchpole.' Everyone was dead serious. 'Dall it, I thought that one on the right would knock that one over on the left.' Emma sat there looking sorry for herself and sorry for Harbourmaster Bill. This went on for an hour or so and if one of the company dared to laugh at him, Bill reached the gun down off the two cart nails driven into the beam below the mantelpiece and there was a hasty retreat from the scene. On one of these drinking bouts, which lasted rather longer than usual, he had bills printed of a sale of his live and dead stock. He got his neighbours to come all dressed up and provided plenty of refreshments, he himself acting as auctioneer. He sold all his stock, knocking every lot down to himself. Frank Wheatcroft saw this with his own eyes and said, 'It's the certain truth and the truth needs no study.' One of the small bunch of neighbours laughed at Bill and was lucky to escape uninjured, the gun riddling the stable door as the man made a hasty retreat.

In a way this is all so sad, such a pity, but it's life, and although people like the Harbourmaster have lived and died in our towns, they are so much less in evidence than if they lived in our country villages. Bill never injured anyone; his last fling as far as I can gather was when he chased an imaginary figure through Howard Cambridge's ten-acre field of brussel sprouts clothed only in his nightshirt and wielding a carving knife. After this, Emma bought Spud a car and Spud took them to market, sometimes venturing as far as Gloucester and Worcester, calling at an old posting house in Pershore on the way to Worcester (or Ooster) cheese fair. Bill told the barmaid to be quick getting him a drink as he was going to Ooster and the 'ship sails at twelve o'clock'. The barmaid was nonplussed—she knew Bill as an old harbourmaster, and told the landlord: 'Bill Charlton is going to Worcester and says there's a ship that sails at twelve o'clock. I didn't know that ships sailed from Worcester.' Out in the bar Bill explained that he was going to Worcester to buy some ship (sheep) and they started selling them at twelve o'clock.

As I pass Appleton Dock, a flat, grassy platform with perhaps a pleasure cruiser tied up there, I think of the Harbourmaster, long since laid to rest in his native Appleton churchyard. He was perhaps the smallest harbourmaster (self-styled) in these islands. I wonder whether he ever saw the sea. The Wren's Nest is now a housing estate and no more to be seen are the heaps of cider apples mellowing under the gnarled trees in Gossle Orchard.

CHAPTER TWENTY-THREE

OUR VILLAGE FIELD NAMES

WHAT'S IN a name? A rose by any other name would smell as sweet. Ah, but the names of our fields, like house names, do give them character. A shrewd landowner about the turn of this century altered 'New Farm' to 'Manor Farm'—you will agree it gives it status.

At the enclosure of 1773 you may or may not know that bigger lots of land were divided into fields. The usual practice was first to dig a ditch for drainage, this also being the boundary. Then the owner of the ditch planted a hawthorn hedge on his side to keep his stock in. When you see a hedge and ditch alongside, the hedge is not the boundary but belongs to the owner of the ditch, which is on his neighbour's side of the hedge. The hawthorns were usually planted on the bank of soil dug out when the ditch was first made.

The larger tracks of land already had ancient names but on enclosure other names were given to the smaller fields. Some of the field names in our village are uninteresting and commonplace, yet others, which only date back to 1773, are humorous and even sarcastic. Our forefathers did indeed have a keen sense of both humour and sarcasm.

Land ploughed by oxen was ploughed in furlongs or furrow longs, 220 yards being the distance an ox was expected to walk without resting. In our village we get fields called Clay Fluss or Clay Furlong; Ten Fluss or Ten Furlongs. Some districts ploughed their fields in shots. No doubt this is where the expression 'Doing one's shot' originated, meaning doing one's share. The Pikings are known as 'gores' in this area; the rectangular parts of the field were ploughed and the 'pikings' are the odd shapes which were left for grazing. Calves Gore, a low-lying field near the brook, at one time gave me the feeling that at some period in our history a calf had been killed and dressed to be eaten by the family of some returning prodigal son, but 'gores' are triangular shapes, still so called by dressmakers;

Calves Gore is an awkward-shaped meadow and the name suggests that it was grazed by calves.

If we compare field names on old farm maps, it soon becomes clear that the spelling changes over the years. The dialect of our people so often changed the name of a field when grandfather, father and son all pronounced it slightly differently. The Dean from the Old English *denu*, a valley, is still known by the old folk as 'the deun'; 'the Broadenum' is simply the Broad Ham, a ham being a meadow by a brook or river—in our case it adjoins Carrant Brook.

In the West Midlands many of the fields are ridge and furrow ploughed. In some cases the furrows are so deep that a man standing in one cannot be seen by another standing in the next. The lands vary in width and length and usually curve slightly at the headland near the hedge, the reason for this being that the team of oxen drawing the long plough started turning and curved the last few yards of the furrow.

People have different ideas as to why fields were landed up in ridges. Some say to get more land, because undulating fields are larger than flat fields; some say for drainage; some say that it is a leftover from the strip cultivation practised before the enclosure. I have cut a little corn with a bagging hook—a large sickle and pick thank (a wooden hook to hold the standing corn and bring out the sheaf). This was just what we called 'cutting the road round' for the binder or reaping machine. Imagine cutting corn on ridges, by standing on the side of these 'lands', swinging the hook towards the furrow bottom. There would be a certain saving in backbending and the cut sheaves stooked on top of the ridge would dry out better, catching the breeze and sun. It is just a thought, prompted by the experience that our ancestors when they did any job on the land always had a purpose in view.

Eight Luns (or Eight Lands) is one example of our many fields landed up in this way. There are eight lands in this field today—a long narrow field by the school. On the parish boundary lies a meadow known as 'the Butts', it just means abutting a boundary; the adjoining field—the Meers—has a pool and that would explain the name. Next to the Church, Lammas Hey was common pasture but enclosed from Lammas

(August 1st) until the spring.

Let's consider some of the old names given to larger pieces of land. The Thurness is twenty-two acres and its name is derived from the Old English *thurs*, a Giant, and *Ness*, nose shaped. The Thurness is shaped like a giant's nose and is well named.

Who would like an address 'Catsbrain'? One of my fields is graced by such a name. In parts of Buckinghamshire, the word describes a mixture of clay and stone or chalk, and the field is just that, no doubt named in the dim and distant past by a gentleman from Buckinghamshire.

Church or Glebe land has interesting names. Hells Acre used to be Church property and is well described. It is stiff, heavy clay and, until the introduction of the crawler tractor, enough to break a man's heart. The Rope Ground is two acres and the produce provided bell ropes for the village church. The ringers must have rung with enthusiasm to warrant a field for that purpose. We, like lots of villages, have the Slad or Slade—a low flat valley. 'The Stocking' puzzled me for a time; it's just over the hedge from my land. A squarer field it would be difficult to find—in fact nothing like a stocking. Of course 'stock' means a wood, as in stockade, and as The Stocking lies next to Wood Piece we can assume it was also wooded at one time. Big and Little Hollbrook are divided by a brook in a hollow and a hundred withy trees. These drink most of the water in a dry summer. *Hol* is Anglo-Saxon for a hollow.

Near the Lower Deviation Saltway, the names of the fields must go back hundreds of years. I dare not venture to give the meaning of them all—Nosterns Well Piece, Hells Hole, Saltway Piece, Saltway Barn Piece and Coppice, Throughters, Mill Heys, Little Worral, Ellecampane (a local name for a plant or herb).

In a field called Winds End, three parts of the way up Bredon, overlooking the Saltway, is what is known as The Horse Camp. The Horse Camp is a round hollow of about half an acre, like a sunken stadium. Around the grass perimeter an earthen wall can still be seen. When wild animals and hostile tribes roamed our hill, the horses were kept safely in the Horse Camp, their owners keeping patrol of the perimeter all night long. The Wodens is a field quite near, just off the Saltway. The

Anglo-Saxons attributed the great earthworks to Woden, the god of the dead. This is possibly a burial ground; the Lower Grave Hill lies on the other side of the Saltway.

The next field interests me—the Starn Hill. This springs from the same source as the Saren Stones of Stonehenge, the Sarn Rocks in Merionethshire where in Welsh it means a pavement or seat of judgment. There could be a mosaic pavement up there; the Romans were fond of these. The 19th Chapter of St. John reads: 'When Pilate therefore heard that saying he brought Jesus forth and sat down in the judgement seat in a place that is called the pavement.' The pavement is literally a stone pavement set in an open court where the chair of judgment was set.

The Cow Ground seems commonplace but in some tenancy agreements, cows, that is milk cows, were only permitted by the landlord to graze certain fields, the idea being that they impoverished the land, their dung, unlike that of beef cattle, being valueless, the goodness going into the milk.

Then we have the Groaten, an old Roman site and about the only field where Roman coins have been found. Van Diemen's Land no doubt has a history of the last century when so many men were transported there; it lies just below The Stocking. Hundred Acres must have belonged to someone with a sense of humour—it is only half an acre! The publican kept his horse there for years. Klondike is a far cry from the Gold Rush; like Hells Acre it is heavy, sticky clay soil but did grow good asparagus. Next to Klondike is Bunkers Hill which suggests a connection with the American Civil War.

Pinchloaf is a field where stood a cottage once occupied by a dishonest baker who gave short weight.

When I first knew Cinder Meadow there was no doubt in my mind of its origin; so many of our heavy clay fields had parts of the topsoil burnt so that the land was more workable, but how easily can we be wrong! Cinder Meadow started as Set Asunder Meadow, then Sunder Meadow, meaning a meadow which was set asunder from the rest of the farm; it is several fields away from the rest of Deades Charity Farm. The Barn Ground—no one could remember a barn there, but I ploughed it in 1955 and we hit the foundations which reminds me of Robert Leighton's lines on Liverpool:

'We have Castle Street, but castle none.
Redcross Street but its legend who can learn.
Old Hall Street too we have—the Old Hall gone.
Tythebarn Street but no barn.'

Tourists come to our country because of its history and because life is different. England has been described as a patchwork quilt from the air, but owing to mechanisation and the need for our farms to be even more productive, hedges are being bulldozed up everywhere to make room for the heavy implements. When hedges go, the identity of our fields goes too and I thought it urgent that some of the more interesting field names in our village be retained. As we hover on the brink of the Common Market, our weights and measures are sure to go too; five and a half yards will no longer be one rod, the rod that drove the oxen; and a cricket pitch, will it still be a chain of twenty-two yards? The fact which strikes me is that in 1773, enclosure came to conserve our land and now the reverse is happening so quickly before our eyes. I am concerned about this but take comfort from the fact that it is doubtful if the walls will go from the delightful Cotswolds.

CHAPTER TWENTY-FOUR

THE PARISH LANTERN

THE MOON has had so much attention paid to it by writers that there must be very little unwritten and very little unsung about it. When we talk of the Parish Lantern it is the full moon we think of most of all.

It is quite fantastic how great a part the moon played in the everyday lives of the older, more conservative type of market gardeners in the Vale. They planted their seeds when the moon was waxing or getting towards the full; it was reckoned the seeds grew much more slowly if they were planted at the wane of the moon. A ring round the moon meant that wind and rain was on the way.

I suppose pig killing has been a sort of ritual since time immemorial. To kill a pig when the moon was waning, according to my Uncle George, was asking for trouble. He told me quite seriously that 'All the bacon from a pig killed on a waning moon would just fry away in the pan. Watch the moon, my boy,' he told me, 'allus kill your pig when he's waxing.' He told me something quite different about the moon one night: 'Look yonder, there's the old moon in the new moon's arms, and if ever you do see a moon on his back, he's filling with water and presently he ull tip it over us.'

My gamekeeper friend related to me only the other day a story concerning the moon. 'Me Uncle Joe from Hampshire was staying with me along with me Cousin Jim,' he said. 'We had our tea after a cold February day. I had killed a pig and the missus had made some faggots. Well, young Jim, after a tot or two of my home-made parsnip wine, said, "What about a go with the long hundred and twenty yard rabbit net tonight?" My Uncle Joe, keeper on a big estate, answered, "It's no use tonight, it's a full moon." I said, "Wait a minute, I know just the spot on Bredon, the top of Doctor's Wood." Now, Master Archer, you have heard of people getting in the shade of the sun?'

I said I had many times when the old maids (horse flies) are biting and it's glaring down in the July hayfields, and I did hear how they fried an egg on the Prom at Weston.

'Well,' said Gamekeeper Camden, 'that night we got into the shade of the moon. The spot I told you about was alive with rabbits and with three quiet spaniels to drive them, we netted sixty-three at one draw on the slope of the hill and when we walked to the top with our bag, the moon shone as bright as day. You could read a newspaper almost.' I had never heard of anyone getting into the shade of the moon before.

CHAPTER TWENTY-FIVE

THE CHURCH AND THE GRAVEDIGGERS

THE CHURCH once housed the village school and in the gallery the village orchestra with flute, bassoon, drums and cellos made a joyful noise unto the Lord. Lofty read the psalms from the bottom tier of the pulpit and over the pulpit was a sound board. For eighty-nine years Lofty lived in his thatched black and white, wattle and daub cottage. Besides making ladders, he made hurdles and gates. He was born in 1858 and his memory was very good. One of his recollections was of an old villager telling the parson he was like the finger post, 'He points the way, but never goes there.'

Being the chief ringer, Lofty led the way as the team went round the houses at Christmas singing their quaint carols, starting with:

'We, the Ashton ringers, approach at your door,
We can handle our bell and ring you a score,
There's Dodge, Bob and Single, and likewise Extreme.
When Treble man calls, then Treble man leads.'

Tommy No-toes, from the hamlet of Paris, was a bell ringer, clock mender and a bit of a poet. He got his name from losing his toes by frostbite in a severe winter. Some of his expressions linger, a favourite being, 'Shine 'em, break 'em, loaf 'em, bowl 'em and peck 'em. A wing of a chicken is excellent nice pickin'.'

In a part of the funeral service are words which go something like this: 'Man that is born of woman hath but a short time to live and his life is full of trouble.' Scientists tell us today of the million of years this planet has been populated; in the light of this, how short is our stay here. Without being morbid, the fact remains. It has seemed to me over the last few years that gravediggers are a sort of race apart; they have certain characteristics not found in the ordinary manual worker. First and foremost, they have their own peculiar sense of humour, then, they are invariably fairly heavy cider drinkers, and it may be coincidence, but the ones I have known have been, with a single exception, short, stocky men.

Ted was gravedigger in our churchyard when I was a boy. This was a part-time job, of course. Ted was a jobbing gardener most of his time, but as he told me, 'I allus planted um six foot when their time came.' Ted was short, corduroyed, a bit lame and smoked a clay pipe.

'How's thee father?' he asked my friend as we watched him throw the blue clay subsoil out of the grave bottom ready to take an old soldier who had fought in the Zulu War.

'Better, Ted,' said my friend.

'And he had better be or else I'll have him in yur,' said Ted.

I doubt if Ted meant to be callous but he had grown up to his job and so had his father before him. We talked to him about the old soldier about to be buried as he sat on a gravestone and drank cider out of a horn cup and ate his bread and cheese and fat bacon.

The churchyard lay alongside the moat and the park field where we played in the holidays. It was my birthday and one of my aunts bought me a football. We played until the funeral. As we leant over the churchyard wall, we saw Soldier Jim carried shoulder high, his coffin covered in the Union Jack, and heard the bugle blow the Last Post. This was education. We were very quiet and after the lowering into the grave, Ted's next office, when the parson said, 'Ashes to ashes, dust to dust,' was to sprinkle some fine earth on the coffin. Ted was not unkind, but uncouth, unlearned and whack, whack, whack, the box resounded as Ted dropped great clods of blue clay on to the coffin. The vicar mentioned this to him, but Ted was unconcerned, saying, 'Old Jim and me a bin pals all our life and he udn't a wanted nothing different. He udn't a wanted me a gone to the trouble to riddle a bit a fine stuff just to go on top of him. Old Jim's alright under that yew tree, I be gwain to lie anant him one day.' And so Ted did, after he had nearly clocked up ninety!

Rasper Elmdon drank rough cider which gave him a colour like a pickling cabbage. He did a bit of bricklaying and small building jobs and was available as gravedigger at two or three churchyards round here. He kept a decent suit in the vestry and earned a bit extra by helping in burials as well. Working in a house, concreting a floor for a widow woman one day, she remarked on the polish of his spade. 'Yes,' he said, 'I a buried over a hundred souls with that spade.'

'Take it out of my house,' said the widow. 'I won't have a tool like that in here.'

Rasper was a terrific eater. He thought nothing of eating two pounds of raw sausage at the pub with his cider. 'Money,' he said, 'is made round and it's got to go round.' He couldn't keep any and had to vacate his cottage and come and live in my stable when he got in arrears with his rent. He put a window in, cooked on a range and kept his decorations up from one Christmas to the next. In this stable next to my house he had a piano and an organ; he could play any tune by ear and many a night I have lain awake when Rasper has returned from the pub in the next village at turned eleven o'clock and heard him go through one Sankey hymn after another, first on the organ and then the piano.

Our neighbouring village churchyard had sandy soil and Rasper earned his money much more easily than on the clay and stone at home. Humour came into it here once again. 'How did you get on today?' I'd ask him when he came to our door for half a dozen eggs which he would demolish at one sitting.

'Well,' he'd say, 'I a buried one and I a throwed two out, [the land had been used for burials before] and the bloke as buried them's yud don't ache any more.'

Albert, now, was younger, but again he was continually muddled with cider. Ted put them in six feet but Albert was different. He had a family of two boys and a girl and when Albert was muddled, the eldest, a girl, did a lot of digging. Albert so often got weary and if he struck a stone, it meant shallow planting. One or two graves were very shallow indeed and the relatives had to heap great mounds of earth and turf to finish his job. 'The undertaker a gin me no mishurments,' he told me, but of course that didn't really stop him from digging the correct depth. No, you have never seen a funeral as it was when Albert was gravedigger. His daughter, after doing a lot of the digging out, was later joined by her two younger brothers, and after the funeral, when the filling in began, he had the whole family down in the grave treading in the moist clay so that he could get most of it back in without having to wheel it away. Frank Wheatcroft met me in the churchyard one afternoon in early spring after an old friend of his had been laid to rest. Frank poked his walking stick through the soft, newly dug mound of earth and tapped the end of the coffin. We stood there silently and Frank, with such a solemn, forlorn look in his eyes, said, 'Fred, that's old George as my stick's hitting now. I reckon he's only in about eighteen inches.'

CHAPTER TWENTY-SIX

BARBERS

'EVEN THE hairs of your heads are all numbered,' so Joe Baker told us in Sunday School at the old chapel as bits of plaster fell from the crumbling ceiling. Joe's hair—white and parted down the middle—shone like polished silver on those Sunday mornings. Joe's wife cut it, always had done since they had married away back in the nineties.

My first recollections of hair cutting were when Dad turned a kitchen chair 'arse bachuds', as Tom Wheatcroft would have said. I sat astride the chair facing the back and Dad put a sheet over my shoulders, tucking it well in around my neck and the rest reached to the kitchen floor. I wouldn't say Dad was an expert but he made a fairish job; the trouble was it did seem to take him an awful long time. As I leant over the chair back, Dad snipped away, combing all the time with a steel comb which scratched my scalp. 'Keep still, will you, fidgitting about, and hold your head upright.' That was only the beginning of his comments. Then he pushed my head to one side and told me to keep it there—which I didn't. The next thing I remember was a periodic blowing down my neck as bunches of hair went under the sheet and tickled beneath my shirt collar. When he got to the nape of the neck, I brought my shoulders up and there he was, struggling to get the scissors into that difficult place and me squirming as he tried. 'Lily,' I remember he once said to Mother, 'just come and look at this boy's head—he's got two crowns.' I really didn't know whether this was a desirable thing or not—the one thing I longed for was the end of the operation. No, he hadn't finished yet; up on the mantelpiece he kept his cut-throat razor—a German one, I believe he paid eightpence—or was it one and fourpence?—for it in Birmingham. He stropped it until it was sharp and tested it by shaving a few hairs off his arm—bare to the elbows with his shirt sleeves rolled up. 'Now don't you dare to move.' This was an order from him to be obeyed. I knew the danger of an open razor. Dad shaved my neck clean, blowing the fluffy bits of hair as he did so and sending cold shivers up my spine. As he took off the sheet and did more blowing down my neck, I knew that the worst was over. From the medicine cupboard he then brought out a bottle of Bay Rum. This puzzled me a bit, knowing Dad's strong views against the drink, but apparently Bay Rum was good for the hair and was very different from the rum from the Indies. He parted my hair on the left-hand side—just the same as it is today, except that mine, like Joe Baker's, is turning silver.

Alf-Fly-by-Night—gardener, cowman, hedgelayer and a man who took jobs by the rip or piecework, cut hair on summer Sunday mornings in his garden. A tall, lean man with a ginger moustache—a man with a memory. Some said he could remember the Crimea. Alf's customers had no need to tell him how they wanted it cut—there was only one style. He operated on the little lawn among the roses in front of his thatched cottage. No, it was not 'short back and sides' but the County Crop. The County Crop, just in case you don't know, is very short all over, a style named after the haircuts in the county jails. Alf left a short stubble—long hair, he said, 'saps your energy'. You could always pick out the ones who had been to Alf's, but every man in our village wore a hat of some sort so the time to pick them out was at home, at church or at Chapel.

Next to Alf's pigsty in his garden was the Drink House, where he stored all his home-made wines and his cider. He made some very good parsnip wine and his customers usually had a drink with him on Sunday mornings. Young Arthur Bradfield fainted while having his hair cut at Alf's and was revived with a tot of parsnip wine. This became a habit of Arthur's and a tot of parsnip wine always revived him.

Alf's gone now. He never cut my hair, but Jack, my friend, and I used to watch the proceedings through the rose bushes.

We had yet one more barber, or hairdresser perhaps we had better call him—Richard Bovey, a retired hairdresser off one of the big ocean liners. The gentry went there by appointment only. My old friend, Tom Wheatcroft, told me he was as false as Judas.

'Why, Tom,' I said 'he seems all right.'

Tom sniffed as if he was on the hill and scented a fox. 'Well, you knows Howard Cambridge has his hair cut there and you also knows as Howard is a student of prophecy, knows his Bible and bides by it.'

'What's that to do with Mr. Bovey, Tom? There's no connection.'

Tom, who had been cutting a kerf of hay with his hay knife in our rickyard, stopped to whet his blade with his rubber. He then put the knife on one side, leaned against his ladder and told me his secrets.

'I'm not denying, Tom,' I said, 'that Howard is a good living man, one of the best, but I don't like to see him sucked in.'

Tom went on, 'Old Bovey keeps a Bible, a prayer book and the Apocrypha on a shelf in the front room of that little brick cottage where he cuts the gentry's hair. He keeps them there especially for Howard and the Parson. He rolls off the scriptures like a saint.'

I was getting more and more curious. 'But there's nothing wrong in that.'

'Unt ther though?' Tom's face reddened as he spoke. 'On another shelf below he keeps the racing papers and studies the form and prices of the race osses and runs a book.'

'Runs a book? What sort of a book?'

'Oi,' Tom said, 'thee ut understand one day—he's an authorised bookmaker, and that unt all, he sells picture postcards as be nothin' but nasty—women a no bodices on. But mark my words, Frederick, he's a gettin' long in the tooth. He left the sea a smart feow years ago and I don't reckon as he ull want many more clean shirts. He's like that town hall clock at A'sum—four faces. No, I likes a mon as is a bit straightforward, one way or the other.'

Tom's final words demolishing Mr. Tovey were, 'I notice thee dad don't have his hair cut there, he goes to Greens at A'sum.'

While I am on the subject of hair cutting, Jasper Hill was too mean to pay the barber. Walt, the carter, said, 'He was that near that if he had a kept a shop he ud a split a carroway seed to get just the right weight.'

One morning Jasper came in the stable about seven o'clock, looking very strange. Walt said, 'Thee looks like a pig a one ear.

What hast thee been doing to thee hair?' Jasper sheepishly replied, 'Oi, the missus started cutting it last night and hadn't got time to finish both sides so her's cuttin' the other side tonight.' Then Walt, turning to his eldest son, said, 'I should think you ul get your hair cut Saturday, I'll be dalled if it yunt as long as Boxer's tail.' Boxer was the favourite Shire in the stable.

Walt's boy was my age and we collected fag cards. We were collecting sportsmen—boxers in particular—Walt got the reply, 'I'm not having my hair cut, I'm training to go backuds like a boxer.'

Frank Wheatcroft's hair was curly, iron grey in colour, with a fringe showing under the peak of his cap. Every six weeks he had the Saturday off from working for Howard Cambridge, took the train to Gloucester for the day together with his wife and daughter and had his hair cut by a woman in Barton Street.

'I be very particular who cuts my hair,' he told me. 'At some of the scruffy places, there's company.' I knew what he meant, the things that Keatings kill. The Gloucester journey was really an excuse for a day out. He described it to me something like this.

'When we gets off the train at Gloucester, we goes to the Monks Retreat—that old pub near the cross. Now you knows as how your Dad got me to sign the pledge and wear the blue ribbon years ago after I had drunk three hogsheads of cider one year?' I remembered. 'Well,' Frank said, 'I have never broke that and all me and the missus has at the Monks is dry ginger. Our Alice and her chap has a stout but that's their business, but down in there, thur's an old organ and when you puts a penny in you gets beautiful music like them steam organs at A'sum Mop.'

From the pub Frank and his family went on to the Bran Mash (Bon Marché), and then dinner at the Occidental (I never found the place). 'The ooman as cuts my hair,' he told me, 'is that there clean you could eat your fittle off the floor and her a got the wi-er-less on. Last wick her sang to it whilst her cut my hair. The song was 'I never tasted kisses until the other night, how long has this been going on'—nothing vulgar, mind, all above board. Then we went to a restaurant and had tay,' he said, 'out of a pot and the last cup as good as the first.'

The next morning being Sunday, Frank stayed in bed. Alice brought him a cup of tea and started the bath water. Cold water was available in the tap but the hot had to be carried from the copper. Then she put some bath salts in ('Does ya good ya know') and then he had his bath and washed his hair. 'That ooman at Gloucester ud a done it but I a sooner do it meself. After me bath the missus comes up with the paper and starts to go downstairs. "I wants you a minute," I shouted. "Thurs no need for me to tell ya what for." Then her brings me breakfast up—a slice of fried, home-cured ham and a shaving of beef off the joint fried in the fat and a couple of fried eggs. "Eat this up, Frank," she says, "it ull do you more good than what's on your mind." Of course, as usual, she was right and I dressed about ten o'clock, put me slippers on and sat in me Berkley chair in the front room. We a got some decent furniture as you can see, Fred, and it's all paid for. I don't believe in this never-never stunt. We have saved a few pounds and you knows I have never robbed our gaffer of a halfpenny and when I meets my Maker, I yunt afraid and we all have got to one day whatever them there scientists says.'

That was Frank's tale of his haircut and what happened after, and he was ready for the land work on the Monday.

CHAPTER TWENTY-SEVEN

THE BALANCE OF NATURE

BOYS LIKE me in the 1920s, living in the country, were in the happy position of never even questioning the existence of God. We read in Genesis, chapter one, that at the close of the sixth day, God saw everything that he had made and behold it was very good. How literally this mystery was acceptable to us varied as we grew and our character developed. The important thing that we inherited from the old and staid villager was that behind everything which went on in the countryside around us was a master hand—some people called it Providence. We believed when the November-planted wheat took perhaps six weeks to come up and the late April-planted barley shot through the warm earth in forty-eight hours that nature was not just an accident but the plan repeated itself from one Christmas Day to another.

Ruskin was considered by some as one of the oddities of the last century. He made mistakes, but don't we all? Some of his theories hold good today. He said, 'To watch the corn grow or the blossoms set, to draw hard breath over the ploughshare and spade, to read, to think, to love, to pray, these are the things that make men happy.' I can picture Dad returning from the hot July hayfields, his flannelette shirt soaked with sweat, hay seeds in the rim of his straw hat collected from roping the last waggonload of hay for the day as the darkness fell, sitting over supper and Mother saying to him, 'You've overdone it again.'

'More people rust out than wear out,' Dad told us as he experienced the indescribable enjoyment of his well earned supper, his armchair and evening paper. Did ever a Lord Mayor's banquet equal this? You see, he had the secret of being at peace with the world of nature—at peace with his fellow men and trusting in Providence—at peace with himself.

The dust which settles on the heart is so much more soul destroying, does so much more damage than the dust which settles on the mantelpiece over the fire. Doctors today have found out how important it is for the natural body, the mind, the spirit, all to co-ordinate and have proved beyond doubt that it's care, worry and anxiety, not work, that kills.

Regarding the so-called Balance of Nature, we all realise that man has been obliged to upset this to a certain extent ever since he has been on earth. Nevertheless, ignorance of natural laws and misunderstanding of them can lead to disasters, for example, dustbowls, plagues and deserts.

There has been an enormous increase these last few years in the spraying of farm and garden crops. Do not think that I am against all spraying, all artificial fertilisers and all that science has done—especially in the veterinary field, but in some cases sprays have been harmful to bird and insect life. Birds discriminate, sprays do not, and along with the greenfly they can kill the birds and insects which do good. Field beans in Norfolk doubled their yield when hives of bees were placed in the field to assist pollination. The killing of weeds by weed killers which are in most cases non-poisonous has resulted in other weeds taking their place. Onions cleared of chickweed and groundsel by calcium cyanide—which is a fertiliser for grass—has resulted in the field soon becoming a meadow. Ragwort is a poisonous weed if eaten by cattle, but they won't eat it unless it has been sprayed with weed killer, then it becomes palatable and dangerous to stock.

In this balance of nature story you can call me 'middle of the road'. We just cannot afford to abandon all that the agricultural chemist has produced—some things have been a God-send, but on the other hand the need to be more selective becomes greater every year.

Wood-pigeons have increased in numbers and are Public Enemy No. 1 to the farmer. Gamekeepers shoot and trap every bird and animal which attacks pheasants and partridges; owners of woods won't allow organised pigeon shoots to start until February 1st when the game-shooting season ends. By February 1st, the time of year has got rather late to shoot the pigeon as he returns to roost at dusk, filled with sprouts, clover and other greens. Thousands, as they return, have filled their crops to such an extent that as they fall dead from the trees, shot from hides in the wood, their crops often burst on impact with the ground. The Ministry of Agriculture had been giving a shilling for each tail of grey squirrels and cheap cartridges to help to lessen their numbers. It was then discovered that grey squirrels raided wood-pigeon's nests and destroyed the young. Payment has been stopped, with the result that there has been an increase in the number of grey squirrels, but fewer pigeons. The grey squirrel is not a native but, although vicious and cruel, he does help to keep the balance of nature.

Isn't nature cruel? Think for a moment of the way a cat worries a mouse until he finally kills it. A Keatings' advertisement used to say, and very true it was:

> 'Big fleas have little fleas
>   Upon their backs to bite 'em,
>   Little fleas have lesser fleas
>   And so ad infinitum.'

I have already said that in doing their job, gamekeepers kill birds of prey and recently the Worcestershire plum growers, having had so much damage done to their plum blossom, have asked that hawks and owls be put on the protected list of birds. These birds have become so scarce that the bullfinch population has built up so that what was once a rarity can now be seen in great numbers—and how pretty they are. Such a pity they do so much mischief. Rooks do damage but also eat millions of wireworms and leather jackets.

The partridge population is largely governed by the sort of weather we get in May and June. If the clay ground is wet and the clay balls on the feet of the young chicks, they get bogged down and killed by vermin. I found an English and a French, or Red Legged, partridge nesting together last year. They hatched a good brood between them and it did strike me whether there would be any language difficulty or whether they talked in Pigeon English! Sometimes a hen partridge will lay in two nests and make the cock bird sit on one lot of eggs. I like the partridge. He is native to this country and it is pleasant to hear his metallic call on a foggy November late afternoon as the coveys are about to settle for the night in the burra, as we say, or to be more precise in a grassy furrow deep between the lands or ridges of our West Midland counties. The droppings left over-night, Oliver, our rabbit catcher, called 'their postcards'—very apt, I thought.

Pheasants, there is no need to say, practise polygamy. They are one of the few birds who have several wives and the instructions at the last shoot of the season are to 'shoot the cock birds only'.

Myxomatosis killed ninety-eight per cent of our rabbits in 1954. There was much hand clapping among both the Ministry and the farmers. You no doubt saw, as I did, the swollen heads of the blind rabbits killed on the roads in thousands. The eyeball bursts with pus, then the rabbit goes deaf and loses all sense of direction. Its sex organs swell. Crows and magpies would pick out its eyes while it was still alive. The Ministry said it was not a cruel death but can one imagine anything more barbaric and unchristian? It was spread by man first of all and then by fleas.

No one seems to know when the rabbit came to these islands. It may have been here when England was joined to the continent of Europe; some say the Romans brought it and introduced the ferret to catch it. The first reference to ferreting was in Spain 50 B.C., by a weasel type of ferret from Africa. The rabbit has always been the countryman's quarry—the cottager's Sunday dinner, the shooting man's standby, the poacher's joy. He destroys trees, garden crops and corn but he is cheap meat and sport. Up until 1880 tenant farmers were not allowed to kill rabbits, but an Act of Parliament was passed making it legal owing to crop damage. Yet I have seen a hundred rabbits killed in a cornfield which yielded a ton of grain to the acre—a good yield in the 1930s.

Oh yes, rabbits were tasty during the meat rationing for the farm workers. Now, fed in large units, rabbits are being bred extensively on expensive purchased feeding stuffs, which does not make sense to me.

Hares have also increased in numbers since the disappearance of the rabbits. Badgers have had to change their diet, now eating quite a lot of fruit, notably damsons, but they have also turned their attention to the nest of the wild bumble bee to get the wild honey. This bee is the only one that can pollinate certain types of clover and farmers are finding it difficult to seed their clover because of the absence of bees.

Nineteen sixty-seven was notable because of the absence of wasps. 'Jolly good,' say the fruit pickers, but there has been a plague of crane flies or daddy-long-legs. Wasps live partly on these things and the absence of wasps will mean a build-up in the population of leatherjackets—the larvae of the crane fly. One crane fly produces 300 leatherjackets, so the balance of nature goes down with a bump in favour of the leatherjackets.

We have often heard the expression 'he is sowing his wild oats' but wild oats come up without being sown at all—just one of nature's unsolved mysteries. A field sown to grass for five years or more then ploughed and planted with pedigree seed will have wild oats with the wheat, the seed having lain dormant in the ground for years.

When bomb craters resulted in the subsoil being thrown up from a great depth, many people will remember the blossoming of the yellow Charlock; the Rose Bay Willow Herb, also known as Fire Grass and the Ragwort, all brought forth from dormant seeds triumphant under the June skies—a sort of derisive victory over man's stoutest endeavours.

Are we completely satisfied with the way our food is produced today? First of all, let me say that milk is infinitely cleaner and safer than it has ever been. But some sprays worry me. Newmarket trainers will only buy oats for their valuable horses if they have not been sprayed with chemicals. Are you satisfied with the way broiler chickens are produced? Never seeing the sun, crowded together, dosed with antibiotics and killed at eight or ten weeks, devoid of all taste. Compare the free-range Light Sussex cockerel, brought up on the stubble, finished on barley meal and potatoes, and nine pounds of wholesome meat at Christmas.

We need not go into the artificially caponised cockerels except that the necks of them, when fed to mink, turn the mink sterile. Experts tell us that the pale-yolked efforts called battery eggs have the same food value as free-range eggs with golden yolks. Are they happy in their cages? This is debatable, but there is no doubt about the end product. The tomato growers of this country have ruined the flavour by concentrating on high production and over-watering. I can get tomatoes with a wonderful flavour from one grower who is too busy with his other work to water his greenhouse often; they are so different to the skins of seeds and water one so often gets. Life today has become so artificial, we tend to pamper ourselves too much with car heaters, electric blankets, etc.—all very good for the delicate and elderly, but there is a real danger of our becoming a nation not unlike the broiler and the greenhouse plant.

I read where workers in factories strike when the temperature drops below sixty degrees; Wordsworth never studied the weather or consulted the doctor. He studied in the fields. For us to strike a balance in our lives, we need more than the animals. We need food for the spirit, religion, literature, art and music.

Shakespeare said that, 'The man that hath no music in himself, nor is not moved with concord of sweet sounds, is fit for treasons, stratagems and spoils.' There are exceptions to this theory. Dr. Johnson was once told that a piece of music was difficult and he replied that it was a pity it was not impossible.

There is music in nature. The song of the birds, the whisper of the leaves, the ripple of water on the sandy shore, the wail of wind and sea, the cawing of rooks—song is the companion of the labourer, the boatman, the shepherd, the miner, the ploughman. It has been described as the Mother of Sympathy, the handmaid of religion. The bride goes to her wedding, the labourer to his work, the old man to his long, last rest, all accompanied by the appropriate music.

The domestic man who loves no music better than the sound of his own kitchen clock and the tune the logs sing on his hearth has something which others never dream of.

When we really retire into ourselves and think deeply of the nature and its fine balance around us, we can call up what memories we please.

CHAPTER TWENTY-EIGHT

THE LONG PLANTATION AND THE DEER PARK

HUMPHREY, THE young squire, still spent most of his time at the Manor and as he prospered both with his estate and in the City he bought yet more land. The Long Plantation was a farm of about six hundred acres to the south of our village. This he acquired on the death of Sir George Cash who had kept it mainly for its shooting value. Rough and bramble-covered it was; Oliver, that wily old rabbiter told me, 'I udn't be surprised to see anything come out of them coverts, I dare say it's amus the same as it was when wolves roamed Bredon.' The Deer Park to the north had belonged to a famous general and was also a sporting property. Humphrey put Roland in sole charge of the Long Plantation and managed the Deer Park himself. Roland farmed the hundred acres or so of land which were still free from scrub, bramble and gorse. He had as his foreman a wiry little bandy-legged ex-yeomanry man, Morgan Jenkins by name. Morgan could handle a horse and had won races in the saddle in the Middle East. While he was managing the Long Plantation for Roland, he rode around those rugged acres on K.B.O.— just his sense of humour, short for Keep Buggering On. K.B.O. stood seventeen hands and Morgan, a slip of a man, won the Amateur Riders Steeplechase at Cheltenham. But Morgan didn't do all his farming in the saddle; at hay and corn harvest, K.B.O. was tied to a five-barred farm gate leading into the harvest field while Morgan pitched and loaded the hay and corn with the farm men. At shows and fairs there are often prizes for the largest potatoes, the longest runner beans and so forth; well, Morgan's speciality was mangold wurzels. Now mangolds grow in two shapes mainly; the round turnip-like globe variety, often golden or yellow in colour, and the tankard, usually red topped and tankard shaped standing halfway out of the ground when full-grown. Seedsmen for years have given cups and prize money for the farmer who grew the most tons of mangolds per acre and Morgan, with his land plastered with as much farmyard manure as the plough would bury, grew mangolds which attracted the attention of farming folk all over Gloucestershire and Worcestershire. I believe he topped about eighty tons per acre one year and it was a foregone conclusion who would win the cup. 'Mangolds,' Harry Read the gamekeeper said. 'When the men went to cart them to the bury with the farm carts, they put one root in each corner and one in the middle and I'll be dalled if they hadn't darn near got a load on. I'll tell tha summat else as Morgan done one year. Mind, Roland let him have his yud over this, he gave him plenty of scope. You see Roland had got to make a good show for Humphrey when he rode over on his hoss about once a wick.' Harry spat as he took his pipe out for a minute, then turning to me said, 'I specs you reckons you 'a sin some crops a wheat.' I said, 'I suppose I have.' Harry came closer and looked around him like so many gamekeepers do—sort of on his guard—then he spoke in low whispers. 'Have you ever sin a ground a wheat when the stooks be so close together that the waggon couldn't get through the gate to fetch the first load?' I had to confess I'd seen no such miracle. Harry went on: 'It was in the summer of 'twenty-one, devilish hot. Morgan planted Square Yuds Master wheat after mangolds down Pigeon Lane. It got a bit winter proud—you understands my meaning—growed longish by early spring. Morgan allus said as a sheep's fart is as good as a cow's turd and he turned the sheep on the wheat. Ewes in lamb they was—Cotswolds. Linseed cake was about six pounds a ton at the station and he stuffed plenty into them yows.' Harry's pipe had gone out and he relit it, puffing smoke as he spoke.

'Roland got the wind up proper, the ground was as bare as the turnpike road by April Fools' Day and he kept Humphrey away for a wick or so, then, Master Archer, didn't that start and stool out like blackcurrant bushes and as green as emerald. That wheat grew taller than the hedges—almost as tall as the gate and lucky we had a hot dry summer. Three hosses and the binder cut it August Monday and I helped to stook it. Harry said we put the stooks in rows like the aisles of the church, just leaving room for the waggon, but it was so thick on the ground by the gate we had to put another row of stooks across the gateway.'

'Well, what happened?' I said, itching to know.

Harry gave me such a look then, he said thoughtfully, 'You beun't a gwain to take the rise out of me if I tells ya?'

'No,' I said. 'This is something quite interesting, out of the ordinary.'

'Well, Humphrey rode over along of Roland and Morgan brought three men with him and they drew the waggon alongside the gateway in the Pecked Meadow. The men got to work with their shuppicks and pitched the sheaves of corn through the gateway to each other and Morgan stood on the waggon and loaded one load of wheat without the waggon ever going in the wheat ground. That's a rum un yunt it,' he said, 'but it's the gospel. I just forget how many load they had out of that ground. When we threshed it Humphrey had all the straw stacked in the boltins in the Dutch barn and kept it for thatching the cottages and buildings. Yes,' Harry said, 'Morgan knowed how to farm and as long as he was about, Roland had it cushy, but of course I only helped a bit at harvest. I was yud keeper at the Plantation and the Deer Park—that's how I damn near got into quod. Harry Read reared his pheasants in long rows of coops under broody hens in the green meadow next to the Long Plantation itself. Never took me clothes off for six weeks after the chicks were hatched,' he said. 'We had a hut up there, me and the boy, and the place was alive of foxes. Humphrey being a keen hunting man said he would sack at a minute's notice any of his men who shot or trapped a fox.' Harry moistened his lips as he told me with relish that 'them two gentlemen—Roland and Humphrey—didn't know how many we killed. We had got to get a good show of birds for the gentry by October.'

Harry told me how Morgan got him a hunting horn which still hangs in his living room.

'Now, Master Archer, you didn't live far from the Long plantation as the crow flies. Now, when the wind was in the south-west, did you ever hear me blow that fellow on the wall' (pointing to the horn) 'in the middle of a summer night?'

I told Harry I had heard it lots of times but never connected it with him.

'You see,' he explained, 'Reynard knows the sound of that

horn and as I walked the woods just after we had put the birds in, I blew it when I heard a stick crackle in the night, or sometimes I saw his eyes shine like a wall-eyed dog in one of the rides.' Harry told me he had heard the Master of the Foxhounds and the huntsmen blow and give Reynard the music—sometimes it was 'Gone Away', 'Breaking Cover' or 'Gone to Ground'—in fact, the lot. 'It done the trick, mind, he sloped off out of our plantation, away from the young pheasants into a nearby coppice, but it was no good thinking of bed, that had to wait until all the birds could roost.'

Humphrey was proud of his deer in the Park. 'Bin there since Queen Bess's time,' Harry said. Humphrey walked the Park when the fawns were born in the bracken and Harry and the underkeeper marked what they caught young. Another very important job Harry had was to castrate a number of the buck deer. 'But why, Harry?' I said. 'Humphrey, you knows, liked venison for the gentry all the year round. Why castrate them, Harry?'

Harry sniffed and gave me a sympathetic grin. 'Stags or bucks stinks like boar pigs in the rutting or mating season and unt good grub. If you was to eat some, Master Archer, that ud grind like sand between your teeth. Humphrey doctored some young stags and when he wanted some venison, the man you be talking to had to shoot one with a Lee Enfield 303 what Humphrey bought off the General. I'd then dress him a castrated young stag known as an Avion and that made good grub for Humphrey and his friends.' Harry told me the lot—'Interesting times,' he added. 'I well remember I had to shoot one Avion every August 15th to hang as long as the first week in September when eighty bell ringers and friends sat around a hunch of venison at the Annual Bell Ringers' Supper. That was in Rev. Havelock's time—Cambridge Blue at Boxing, did you know him?'

'Ah, I remember him, a humorist and singer at village concerts.'

'That's him,' said Harry. Harry thought a bit, then said something quite different. 'You ud allus reckon a parson to be a bit of a pansy, a tea drinker, a bit of an hot-house plant.'

'Well,' I said. 'Some may be.'

'Master Havelock was different when he first come to the village, middle aged. Some chaps got whistling and calling after him. He called them back and asked them what they wanted and when they said nothing, he gin um all a darn good hiding, oh yes, he could use um.'

Squire Humphrey thought a lot of Harry, the keeper, and employed a young chap named Dick Smith, who lodged in the village, to help out with the game at the Deer Park and the Long Plantation. Dick took to the cider and oftentimes roamed the hill at night the worse for drink. The road, or ride, to the Park went through the village churchyard. Once Dick walked up from the pub after closing time to look around the Park, and close by the pathway the sexton had dug a grave ready for a funeral the following morning. Getting a bit off track, ass over yud Dick fell into the open grave. There was not enough power left in Dick's muscles to enable him to climb out, so he rolled himself up in his overcoat and slept the night in the open grave. As dawn broke over the Cotswolds and the earliest of the birds started their song in the churchyard yews, Dick heard footsteps coming down from the Park. Harry told me that when you are underground you can hear all footsteps in the field you are in. If you listen with the stock of a muzzle-loader gun on the ground and put your ear to the end of the barrel—a dangerous practice—you can hear footsteps clearly.

'Like a doctor's stethoscope,' I said.

'You got it,' said Harry.

As the footsteps drew near, Dick popped his head out of the grave in the morning half light and shouted, 'What time is it?' The man dropped the sack bag he was carrying and ran for his life. Dick eventually got out of the grave and was interested to see what was in the bag. A poacher had left him fifteen rabbits and twenty-five snares. Dick told Harry that with rabbits at tenpence each he had a better night than he expected.

Being well used to dressing deer to provide venison for Humphrey's dinner table Harry naturally killed a pig or two in the winter time. Fred Simpson kept a few pigs in an orchard close by Humphrey's lake or fish pond which bordered the flower garden and shrubbery from the Park. 'Gloucester Old Spots they were,' Harry told me. 'They were good doers but the sword [rind] of the bacon was thick.' Fred's boar was old and had nasty tusks nine inches long. One spring morning after Fred and Harry had had a conflab as to the best way of dealing with this now dangerous boar pig and decided he would be best placed in a Birmingham sausage factory, Harry prepared for the slaughter. After coaxing this huge twenty-score animal into Fred's stable with its low door, Harry planned the operation. He got Frank Wheatcroft to make a noose with strong waggon rope, cut an apple into pieces and smeared the cut apple on the rope. Harry dangled the noose over the half-door and after one or two sniffs the great boar put his nose in and Harry tightened the rope and fastened the loose end to the top hinge of the door. Harry was at the ready with his 303 Lee Enfield rifle and shot the boar dead centre in the head. He then entered the stable and stuck him and dressed him. Next day on cutting him up he found the bullet had travelled from the skull right down the pig's spine.

'But why,' I asked Harry, 'didn't you kill him the ordinary way with the humane killer?'

'Ah,' Harry said, 'I told you about those tusks. When we approached him first of all he roared at me like a lion. He meant business and if I had have gone into that stable he would have ripped me to pieces. Mind you,' Harry was serious as he spoke, 'it's a job I udn't do again, I likes to do my work the normal way but this was exceptional.'

Roland over at the Long Plantation told Humphrey that one of the fields at the back of some fir trees grew every crop he planted and a bumper crop at that. 'Humphrey,' he said, 'do you mind if I plant about eight acres of late peas?'

'Well, you know,' Humphrey said, 'we aren't exactly market gardeners but please yourself, if you can get the pickers.'

Roland assured Humphrey that the local women would be glad to earn a bit extra and there were always the gypsies. Late peas do well on the hill; the constant breeze prevents them getting mildew—that fungus which discolours the pods. Morgan suggested Lincolns as the best late variety and planted them early in May in a Cotswold wall-enclosed field. The land was in good heart after a crop of swede turnips had been sheeped off in the early spring. Harry led the horse pulling the

drill and Morgan walked behind holding the drill tails and
keeping a straight mark. When the peas came up they were a
picture, the pale green shoots soon turning darker as the first
leaves grew. 'As straight as a die,' Morgan told Humphrey and
Roland when they rode over on their horses. The usual cultiva-
tions took place and by late summer the field was a mass of silver
bloom and the local people were already speculating as to the
yield per acre. Now the field behind the firs was isolated and as
the peas came into pod the rooks, the crows, the pigeons started
on what to them was a feast. Roland was desperate. He couldn't
face Humphrey if the birds had all his peas. Morgan sent one of
Harry's boys up to scare the birds off; early in the morning he
went, then Harry made hides and shot the birds from there, but
regardless of all these things, the birds were winning. Late at
night they fed, and on Sundays, when Harry's boy went up
later in the morning, and Saturday afternoons when no one was
there. Harry Read was a shrewd man but as he told me, the next
move he made very nearly got him in quod (Gloucester Jail).
'Mind you,' he told me, 'the Squire didn't know but I'd
poisoned foxes with strychnine and always kept some in my
hut on the hill, so I said to Morgan, "I want a few bushels of
wheat, I am going to poison them crows".' Morgan sent some
up on the muck-cart. Next day, Harry got to work, got the
wheat just a little damp and mixed it all with strychnine, then
Harry broadcast the grain all over the pea field—just a little
light sowing—washed his hands and went home to tea. Early
next morning, I happened to be in the next field. We had a field
of oats to carry and I went up with Walt and the waggon.
Harry rushed along full of excitement and full of dismay; he
could see that he had made a dreadful mistake. All over the pea
field, and it looked to me more like a battlefield, were dead birds
of all descriptions—pigeons, crows, rooks, larks, plovers, partridges and the odd cock pheasant. The rooks which remained
were flying in circles, 'cider making', Walt said, and dropping at
all points of the compass. The scene was fantastic and put the
fear into me at once.

Harry said softly, 'I suppose I a got enough of that sugar
[that's what we called it] to wipe out all the folk in Ashton.'
Walt said, 'I picked up a rabbit out of one of your wires last

night with his head bit off by a fox, the missus is cooking him for dinner today.' 'He's full of strychnine,' Harry said. 'I planted him for that fox that's having my birds'. 'Run like 'ell, Fred,' Walt ordered me. My legs hardly touched the ground all the way to Walt's cottage at Paris where I told Walt's wife about the rabbit which she had already skinned. Harry told me after, 'That ud a got me into quod as sure as hell's a mouse-trap.'

But back to the birds on the hill. Walt unhooked his filler or shaft horse out of the waggon into a muck cart and we walked the fields around and picked up cart-loads of dead birds and Harry buried them in the Long Plantation thinking no one else knew. A mile and a half away in the next village is an old-established rookery, plum opposite the police station. The rooks trying to come home to roost that night after gorging them-selves with strychnine-dressed wheat were falling flop, flop in the road outside the policeman's garden gate. P.C. Downs was soon up at Morgan the Bailiff's house, asking a lot of awkward questions. Luckily Morgan didn't know a thing, but at the back of his mind he had a feeling that Harry had done something drastic about the birds on the peas—very drastic!

The birds never returned to that field of Lincoln peas and Roland was able to prove to Humphrey the young Squire that he could grow peas for market as well as the Evesham market gardeners. The yield was good, the quality excellent, but little did the Squire know how the birds nearly wiped out the crop and how Harry had dealt with them and nearly wiped out Walt and his family with strychnine.

CHAPTER TWENTY-NINE

JOHN CLOPTON

MY FATHER never referred to a shoe repairer as a cobbler but a 'snob'. In a Georgian brick-built house with its windows darkened by an overgrown yew tree lived John Clopton the snob. The house was roomy; it belonged to Squire Humphrey, together with a large garden and a row of pigsties. John was never married and lived with his sister and brother-in-law who also had practised the art of shoe repairing. No, it's hardly fair to say that as John's brother-in-law, Old Man Hyde, was a shoemaker and made shoes to measure for some of the gentry. John had picked up a certain amount of Mr. Hyde's art after he had done his time in the Army, being pensioned off as a Sergeant-Major. It's good to see an upright man—a man with a straight back—and John's Army training had given him a bearing so different from the followers of the plough. Their backs were often bent by carrying hay, sacks of corn, and holding on to the plough tails over rough ground. Just to see John walk past our house from the station was sufficient to impress anyone that he was no ordinary tiller of the soil. True, he did keep a few pigs and kept a good vegetable garden and when old Mr. Hyde got past mending the shoes of the villagers, John mended shoes for whom he pleased. His Army pension gave him independence. In fact, when he mended shoes for anyone he left him in no doubt that it was a favour.

The easiest way to rile John was to take him a pair of shoes to mend which had been mended by someone else before. Roland had several fine pairs of riding boots and his little servant girl, Elsie, took a pair to be soled and heeled by John. John, apart from his military bearing, had a trimmed military moustache—tobacco stained—and he wore pince-nez spectacles which he peered over when he spoke, all rather frightening for a young girl to approach for a favour. Roland's boots had been repaired before elsewhere and John could see this at a glance. He threw them back at little Elsie shouting, 'Take them to the man who repaired them last time.'

Elsie whispered, 'They belong to Master Roland, a friend of the Squire.'

This infuriated John still more and opening his workshop door he replied, 'Get out, girl, and the boots, I don't care if they belong to the King of England.'

'Passionate,' Tom Wheatcroft called him. 'That unt all as he's passionate with either,' Tom said, 'He cuts the sticks and gets the coal in for Ray Lewes' widda.' Tom's eyes had that wicked glint in them and I knew when Tom added, 'Oi thur's more to it than that,' that John and Mrs. Lewes were possibly a little more than just good friends. 'And what about Mildred at the bottom of the village?' Tom cleared his throat. 'Thur's temptation if you like.'

I said, 'John feeds her pigs.'

'Oi, I know,' Tom said, 'but they dropped out the other day —John and Mildred. You see, John unt at the top of Mildred's list. Master Bosworth with the gammy leg have put John's nose out lately and the other morning when I took the cows back from milking past the drooping ash by Mildred's, Mildred was at the bedroom window. I didn't ketch all as was said between um but I did hear John tell her, "Mildred, I hate you and if I had a gun I'd shoot you." I udn't put it past him neither,' and as Tom said this there was a sort of smile come over his face as much as to say 'good riddance to bad rubbish'.

Tom summed up by telling me, 'Thur's two sorts a passion and bwoth of um wants taking in moderation. Mind tha, John learnt a smart bit out in India.'

A neighbour of mine, a youth in his teens, plough boy for Mr. Cambridge, took his hobnailed boots to John, worn down to the uppers. John swore at him, ran him round the workshop with a horse whip and promised to tell the youth's father about him letting his boots get in such a state. Swearing was probably one of John's worst points. He just didn't care who was about.

Squire Humphrey and Roland were supping their sherry with Rev. Havelock one winter's night at the vicarage and the Vicar said he was much disturbed by the awful language at the Plough and Harrow inn. 'That man, John Clopton—I believe he was a Sergeant-Major in India—is a bad influence on some of the young lads in the village. His language,' said the Vicar, 'is positively disgusting.'

Humphrey and Roland agreed with the Vicar that something should be done about it. 'You can't blame the landlord,' the Vicar added. 'A fine fellow, he doesn't allow any card playing or dominoes on Sundays.'

Humphrey said he would have a word with the landlord and suggest that they have a swear box, a box that every time a swear word was used the offender put a penny in.

'Excellent,' Rev. Havelock said. 'It can go to charity.'

The landlord of the Plough and Harrow agreed and Oliver the rough carpenter knocked up a box out of a few bits of deal wood. To be quite fair, the language improved and a few odd coppers were all that went into the swear box. There was, of course, the one exception, John Clopton. The very thought of a swear box started John swearing. Then John made one of his irregular visits to the pub. He had just drawn his Army pension. 'Moderate your language, John,' the landlord told him as he entered the bar. 'Or else most of your pension will go to charity in the swear box.'

In our village today men still recall that night at the Plough and Harrow. John Clopton started swearing, using every word he could think of, and kept up a constant stream of words for an hour, all the time putting his pennies in the box. He drank beer at others' expense and his fellow drinkers changed his money into coppers just to listen to John's terrible oration. By closing time he had repeated over and over again every word in the book. A short while after, he died from a heart attack and I watched his coffin pass our house on the bier covered in the Union Jack. A colourful character, yes—but he had been a Sergeant-Major.

CHAPTER THIRTY

BOB WITHERS OF STANBOROUGH

SQUIRE HUMPHREY, as you have gathered, had an ambition in life. It was not asking a lot really, just simply that his estate ticked over from one harvest until the next without too many problems. He managed the main estate with the aid of Roland, but farms and estates are not exactly what one sees on picture postcards—there are always the awkward lands, the smaller farms which lie farthest from the village, the farms with rambling, cold houses where life is a constant struggle, coping with stock where the buildings are poor and the water supply dependent on the weather and the distant fields usually in bad heart—neglected by the muck-cart owing to the distance from the cattle yard. These outlying farms Humphrey let to tenant farmers—men who had just put their foot on the first round of the ladder, men who had saved a few pounds after being labourers, which enabled them to pay the moderate rent Humphrey asked for these difficult holdings. Bob Withers was an exception to the usual type who rented the outlying places. Bob had been a dealer, a horse coper, he made cider and sold it wholesale, and in fact, Bob had been a bit of everything including a publican.

In his late sixties, he took over Stanborough from Squire Humphrey—about one hundred and twenty acres near the railway line. Bob himself was a short, stocky, horsy man—muffled and gaitered, a bit of the gypsy in him. He was unwholesome-looking with a blue nose and a bloodshot eye. Bob was a widower with three strong sons and a daughter who kept house for him; a hard taskmaster to his sons and to young Ralph James, who went there as carter and lived in one of the two cottages adjoining the railway line. After he had married, Ralph told me stories of working for Bob as a lad. 'Half past four, I had to be up winter's mornings to git the cows in for milking. Bob was a wicked man,' Ralph said. 'I lived in in them days and I suffered, I can tell tha. He was wickeder than the devil himself. Thirteen, just left school I had.' Ralph raised his eyebrows and puffed at his pipe. 'They udn't stand for it today, mind, and if I could see my time over again, walking the turnpike road with a billycan ud be better than that.' He then went on to describe those winter nights and how he slept in an attic bedroom as cold as charity. 'No candle, mind, old Bob was frightened of fire.' Ralph drew the picture—a thirteen-year-old groping up the attic stairs to a cold bedroom.

'I suppose you had supper, Ralph?' I was hoping that things weren't quite so grim as they seemed.

'Supper,' Ralph retorted, 'if you can call it that. A bit of bread and scrape afore I went up the wooden hill, and breakfast,' he said, 'was always the same, bar Sundays. Six mornings we had cider sop—bread soaked in cider and a bit of bacon on Sunday. I married one Saturday in June—put me frail down in the church porch, tied the knot, and then back haymaking in the afternoon.' But Ralph told me that that was the best day's work he had ever done.

'Our cottage,' he told me, 'was one of the two anant [next to] the railway line, just by Stanborough level crossing.' I know that stretch very well; there is a gradient there perhaps a mile long—not very steep but travelling passenger to Evesham it did slow the train a little. The goods train with a long caravan of waggons behind carrying coal and other heavy goods found Stanborough gradient quite a challenge. So often I have heard when working in the fields a heavy goods train change her tune as she climbed the gradient, then there was the belching smoke, the hissing of steam, and all the time the fireman shovelling in the coal and the driver getting the last ounce out of his engine, coaxing it as it almost talked back at him when the speed reduced to a crawl and the puffs of the loco seemed to be saying, 'I think I can, I think I can,' a longer pause, then 'I think I can.' Ralph's cottage was just past the incline. 'My garden' (he gave me such a wink) 'lay anant the railroad. The drivers were devilish good to me and my missus, they throwed lumps of coal into my garden almost every time the heavy goods passed, and of course I used to throw um a cauliflower or a cabbage, then as they had mastered the incline and picked up speed towards Hinton Station you could yer the old ingin sort a swanking as

her puffed out—"I done it, I done it." Ingins be funny things,'
Ralph said. 'I'd have liked to have worked for the Company
stead of old guts-ache Withers.'

Withers and Humphrey just tolerated one another.
Humphrey would never have let him a farm in the village. Bob
paid his rent but dealt and higgled in the markets and some of
his dealings were looked down upon by Rev. Havelock who
when he knew what a mere pittance he paid his sons and Ralph
James, reminded him of what the Book says, that a servant is
entitled to a just reward.

Bob and Ralph milked a few cows and kept a white shorthorn
bull. Bob's bull was frequently on the railway line and terrorised
the platelayers. Henry-Fly-By-Night, the ganger from the Black
Country, said, 'He mains business and awm a going to tell yow
them shorthorns of 'isn lukes menacing, very menacing in-
daid!'

Bob's idea of buying a white bull didn't quite click. By using
him on his red shorthorns he expected strawberry roan calves. It
didn't happen like that. Rev. Havelock told him 'nature is full
of mysteries'. Bob swore every time a white or red calf was born.
What annoyed him most of all was the fact that neighbouring
small farmers brought their red cows to Bob's bull and got roan
calves. Bob was a good judge of horses and kept a fair team,
although Ralph had to pinch most of the food for them from
the cowshed, saying in his dry sort of way, 'They be having
more mealtimes than meals.' As a widower Bob got around a bit
market days with his high-stepping pony and governess cart.
The pony, Daisy, he bought for five pounds as 'a screw, a wrong
un, a left-handed un' in Gloucester Market. Ralph said 'he
faked her um'. Whatever he did, she went like the clappers and
as Bob sat in the corner seat of his rubber-tyred governess cart,
she fled past our house foaming and still raring to go at the end
of her twenty mile journey from Gloucester which she had done
in something over an hour.

Though Bob was far from good-looking, there was something
about him. He had a fancy for the women as he approached the
age when a working man would be looking forward to his Lloyd
George pension. A young Cotswold farmer and his wife (in
Frank Wheatcroft's words) 'dropped out'. Mary the wife

brought her daughter, Jean, to Bob's house and took the job as housekeeper there. His family had all married and left him, all except Arthur, Ralph describing him as 'not having all his buttons on'. The reaction in our village was a foregone conclusion. The labourers at the pub thought Mary was after Bob's money and Bob wanted a 'lie-by'. Mary, dolled up in her fur coat, wined and dined with Bob and everything in the garden was lovely until Jean went on holiday to spend a week with her father. 'Where does your mother sleep, Jean?' asked her father. 'Oh, with Uncle Bob'—how innocently this ten-year-old Cotswold lass let the cat out of the bag! The Cotswold farmer, a man of similar age to his wayward wife, fortyish, was anxious to get grounds for divorce.

One sunny October day when Bob had just started cider making, the leaves just beginning to fall from the trees in the little orchard at the back of Stanborough Farm, two very ordinary men got off the Birmingham train at our station. They spent the early evening at the Plough and Harrow talking to the locals and inquired where they could borrow a long ladder as they were going to do some roof repairs for Humphrey on Bob's farmhouse at Stanborough. Mr. Stallard, the baker, had a forty-round ladder and lent it to them.

They had chosen a bright moonlight night and took the ladder into the barn by the Plough and Harrow Inn. Long after closing time when everyone had long since gone to bed, the two visitors to our village sat in the barn looking at their watches and keeping very quiet. It's half a mile if it's a yard from the inn to Stanborough Farm and on the stroke of one in the morning they carried the ladder quietly to the farm adjoining the railway. During the day they had made sure from Ralph which bedroom Bob slept in. As they approached Stanborough, a long goods train was labouring up the incline. The men naturally thought this might disturb the sleeping beauties but no, many such trains travelled by night. Somewhere around two o'clock on that October morning, the two strong young men up-ended the ladder and rested the top against the stable roof. Quietly and carefully the ladder was rolled nearer to the dormer window of Bob's room, the window which faced the hill and the village, the other side of the house to the railway track. Like a well-trained steeplejack, the one man mounted the ladder; he had previously changed his shoes and wore rubber gym shoes or pumps. His companion held the foot of the ladder steady while the photographer (for that is just what he was) took a flashlight picture of Bob and Mary sleeping peacefully in the double bed in Bob's room. The graphic report in the local paper set tongues wagging. The Cotswold farmer got his divorce and Bob continued to 'live along with Mary', as we say around here. Bob's gone now. I have a sneaking hope that Mary is enjoying his money.

CHAPTER THIRTY-ONE

THATCHER BUGGINS

GEORGE BUGGINS arrived on the scene in our village just when some of Squire Humphrey's black and white wattle and daub thatched cottages and barns were getting in Frank Wheatcroft's words 'the wuss fur wear'. George travelled up from the Severn side or what is better known as The Berkeley Vale. A short, slight man, wiry and nimble. When he arrived one evening in May on the five-twenty train from Gloucester, the Plough and Harrow seemed to him the most likely place to find lodgings and to get to know a few of the native workers of the soil. The landlord put him up for the night and had been asked by Humphrey to find George some permanent lodgings. There was plenty of work to be found in our village to last George for years. He had, of course, been used to cutting his withies for buckles and spars for the thatch from the banks of the Severn. Willow grows in abundance along those banks where the tow paths form tracks like oversized sheep runs. 'How about withies?' George asked the locals. 'Oi, thee ut find plenty alongside Carrants Brook,' Oliver, the carpenter, told him as he firmly grasped his quart pot of cider. Frank Broadfield, then a young man in his prime, told me that the conversation in the Plough and Harrow that evening was in the main about finding comfortable lodgings for George. 'I'll tell thee what,' Ralph Holmes the plasterer said, 'Thee gu and stop along with Widda Parminter as lives at Coney Hatch with her one little bwoy.'

My old friend, Frank Wheatcroft, told me the whole story: 'Rasper said to George, "Thee ut have a comfortable lodge along with Mrs. Parminter up on the hill in that little cottage amongst the fuzz bushes and plenty of mate [meat] if you wants it."' Frank twinkled his eyes at me and said, 'You know what he means by "mate"?' I understood and out of curiosity asked Frank what sort of a woman 'widda Parminter' was.

'Oh, a big fine, upstanding piece,' he said. 'Her hadn't long lost her man and George fitted the bill nicely.' 'There was nothing went on between them?' I hardly dared ask.

'Bless the bwoy,' Frank chuckled and tapped me on the leg with his walking stick. 'He lay along with her—they cohabited. It ud a bin a pity, Fred,' he said, 'for such a fine piece to just have that one little bwoy.' I almost agreed. 'Well,' Frank continued, 'they (that's George and Mrs. Parminter as was) had eight youngsters afore they married, and ten more arter.'

Up on the hill at Coney Hatch George took a pride in his garden and grew dahlias for show. Every August he showed his dahlias at Bricklehampton flower show and every year Mrs. Parminter showed a new baby—all but once. 'One year her missed, never had a youngster and udn't go to the Show with George. Mind,' Frank continued, 'they lost one or two, allus did in them days, but I'll speak as I find, George Buggins taught young Bill Parminter how to thatch as soon as he left school.' Frank went on to tell me that he couldn't have kept up with George's missus. 'Dall it,' he said, 'when they was harvesting in the Squire's busy time her tied the bands around the sheaves as George cut them and bait time after their bread and cheese and cider, George had to cohabit with her afore her ud start work again. But George kept upsides with her, he had bin in the Merchant Navy for a spell when he was a youth. I expect you have heard about Buggins' Hopper, Fred?' I knew the story. George Buggins sailed around the world in sailing ships and was weatherwise. He could almost smell a storm coming. He told the locals that if you see a cloud in the sky the shape of a hopper on a mill, it's a sure sign of rain within twenty-four hours. 'Look out for Buggins' Hopper,' people still say in this day and age.

Buggins' thatching was a pride and a joy to the village. Humphrey was delighted with him. 'Makes the place look as if somebody owns it,' he said, and of course some of his fancy weathercocks and weather-vanes stood for years, sometimes creaking in the wind for the want of oil.

Now young Bill wasn't worth a hatful of crabs. He started thatching one big barn and had got a little way along the one side and gone through a fair amount of Humphrey's best cider. Old George had packed up thatching now; his old legs weren't safe to carry him up a long ladder. Roland came over with his cob and met Humphrey at the manor, together they watched the pitiful slowness of Bill's thatching and surveyed the long sheep barn. Roland, quite serious, turned to his friend and said, 'Humphrey, I'm not sure what will happen first—whether the barn will fall down or Bill Parminter will finish thatching it.' Weeks afterwards the job was called off. Frank Wheatcroft said, 'It ud 'a broke the bank the way Bill was a going on.' The Buggins family grew up and as Frank said to me, 'You understands nature well, the girls was warm and if I'd got as many sovereigns as times some of the Ashton chaps have seen to them bwoth in the cottage and on the steps, I'd be a millionaire—oi, that I ud be, a millionaire.'

CHAPTER THIRTY-TWO

HEDGES, DITCHES, POSTS AND RAILS

THE MEASUREMENT of land over the years has been done by either estate agents or their like or by what I would describe as amateur land measurers. Tom Wheatcroft told me about the measuring of The New Piece. The auctioneer who was to sell the land made it seven acres, two roods, or seven acres and a half. An Evesham land agent's figures were exactly seven acres. Sam, our local publican, market gardener, and master of other skills and crafts, did land measuring, and he arrived at a measurement of seven acres and a quarter. Sam's measurements were agreed to by both the purchaser and the vendor. The New Piece is still reckoned to be seven acres and a quarter. Such is one aspect of land measurement.

Old country folk, Tom Wheatcroft in particular, stressed the point that this measurement of land included hedges, ditches, posts and rails, which often varied quite a bit with the actual land for grazing or growing crops.

Squire Humphrey's hedges when he took over the estate from his uncle were in pretty good fettle. Admittedly they did include some elm and ash saplings which had overgrown, but they were stockproof.

I have seen many examples of sawn larch rails still sound after forty years' use as fences and stiles. These rails were full of hand-cut nails after stakes had been nailed to them time and time again. They had been sawn by Jonathan, with the first steam operated unguarded circular saw to be seen in our village. This saw eventually cost Jonathan his life when a knotty piece of oak recoiled with a deadly blow to his stomach.

Hedges and boundaries are interesting, essential and can be the source of trouble between neighbours. You see, there has been such a build-up of tradition over the years which varies in different parts of the country. On Enclosure, in our case 1784, ditches were dug as boundaries and the soil thrown up on the owner's land. Some landowners go further than saying they

own the ditch on their neighbour's side; they claim so many feet
on the neighbour's side of the ditch to maintain it. Is is all so
involved, so much bound up in tradition and custom.

The beauty of this is that the true countryman understands
these unwritten laws. As a boy no one told me who owned the
hedges bordering our land until I had a spell as under-stockman
to Tom Wheatcroft. The way he knew at a mere glance how far
our hedges went and, as the ditch suddenly came through into
our side of the fence, our responsibility for fencing, hedgecut-
ting and tree felling ceased, just amazed me. Then he told me of
the Enclosure Act, the Parish Award, and I made it my business
to find out these mysteries of the hedgerows.

One only has to look around and see enclosure disappearing
before our eyes as hedges are ripped up and large acres of land
become one great field. Pastures are divided now by the electric
fence. The advantages are that the land lends itself much more
easily to large mechanisation, the hedges no longer harbour
squitch grass, docks and other undesirable weeds. But the dis-
advantages are clear—no shade for cattle in summer, no shelter
for them in winter; lunches in the hedge bottom, just a
memory; a constant drain on the potential nesting places for
birds, a loss of some of our wild flowers and the fact that
England will cease to be the patchwork quilt of irregular fields,
hedges and trees it has been for two hundred years.

Hedges, ditches, posts and rails have yet another side to their
history; to my mind it is much the most interesting. When
Squire Humphrey, on his uncle's death, inherited the estate, the
Home fields had a quaint, eternal look; they were parkland
virtually, with old gnarled oaks spilt and sprawled, some of
which must have stood in the field overlooking the church in the
time of the first Elizabeth. This field was once the site of a large
moated house, its stream of sparkling spring water, lined with
watercress, supplied the fishpond near the church, and the livestock with drinking water. Tom recalled to me one day how,
when Young Humphrey took over the place, the Home field
had been especially fenced by the old Squire with six rails of
stout larch grown in the parish quarry on the hill. The old man
kept his bulls there in the summer until his death and the sale.
Tom and I were mounding, as he called it (just another name

for fencing), when he said to me, 'I suppose you a never sin a bull twenty-seven year old?' I hadn't. 'Well, what I be gwain to tell ya is the certain truth if I never moves from this yer fence no more. There was only one man could ketch that bull and that was Long Fred Bradfield, a devil of a strong chap. He put a corn sack over his yud. The bull come to him and that was only after he had 'ticed him with some linsid cake. That bull had longer fit on him than I a got and I takes size eleven and he weighed over a ton. Long Fred ketched um all the same road, then led um like a team of 'osses tandem with halters on, all blindfolded, down through Tythe Court to the station after the sale. Mind tha, they was too fat to be much trouble, and they hadn't had no cotter with any of the cows for years. A white un in the bull pen served them.'

'What sort of breed were they, Tom?' I asked. 'Shorthorns?'

'God bless the bwoy, they was all breeds,' he told me as he drove another six-inch nail through a withy pole stopping a gap into the adjoining orchard. 'We never bothered much with pedigree then a day, we judged un by their looks and their performance, when they was all old, specks they went into sausage at Brummingham ... Yes, Frederick, that's wur larch comes in, six rails of sawed larch ull keep anything in bar them deer up in the Park.'

My old friends Tom, Oliver, and the Old Shepherd each had an eye for something useful to be found in our hedges. It takes years of practice to be able to pick out at random pieces of wood or large timber actually growing in the shape to make a particular piece of farm equipment. Now Tom had always been a handyman with a scythe. A scythe sned (handle) has to be a paticular shape. The shape of the sned should suit the man who will use the scythe. Many is the time when Tom has been cutting back an overgrown hedge, or just mending gaps with me, when he has stopped short in his tracks, and said, 'Half a minute you, I a just sin a scythe sned.' Looking at a bent piece of ash I couldn't imagine it growing there among hawthorn. Two or three blows with Tom's hatchet and the ash limb lay at our feet to be shrudded up of its side branches by Tom's sharp bill hook. As this piece of green wood took shape it became clear to me that Tom had cut himself a handle for his scythe. 'That ull

have to be put over the beums under the thatch in the cyart uss
to mella and dry out for a time, then I'll fix him up one wet
day, happen.' No going to town and buying one made of foreign
hickory for Tom. 'A drap of linsid oil on that customer and
he'ull see me through.'

I wonder whether Tom ever thought that by the time his
scythe was completed someone else might be mowing the stinging nettles in the rickyard, the thistles on the Great Hill. I
doubt if ever the thought crossed his mind. If we are really
honest with ourselves we just haven't the patience, the thought
of the future, to wait like Tom for timber to season. Oliver, that
Jack of all trades, looked for so much in our hedgerows. If a
shaft broke on a harvest waggon during the haymaking Oliver
was expected to replace it the same day. He searched the hedges
and the trees for ash bigger and bolder than Tom's scythe sned.
He looked for straight six- or seven-inch diameter stuff at the
butt end, tapering to four inch at the shaft end; this was his habit
all the year round. When he found pieces suitable he shaped
them with his draw knife to match the opposite shaft. These timbers had also to season first. Yes, I can see him now drawing the
staples where the breeching and ridge chain fastened from the
broken shaft and fixing them to his own hand-hewn one.

When the shaft was fixed to the waggon he measured the
width with his rule which he kept in what he called 'the ass
pocket of me trousers'. Then a few more draws with his draw
knife, a rub over with an old rasp, no time for paint, the hay was
ready and waiting. Soon Captain the filler horse was drawing
the waggon again, harvesting the hay, helped by the harvest of
the hedgerows. Then the Old Shepherd would be lopping
withies to make hayracks from the poles for his lambing ewes
and Oliver again cutting the sally or sallow, better known as the
pussy willow which he used for ladder rungs. Crab apple
branches, dried and seasoned, made heads for mallets and
beetles. These could be used without ferrules, the wood didn't
split.

As boys we soon learnt to spot V-shaped nut branches for
catapult sticks. Elderberry, young, straight and pithy, which we
used for pop guns. Granted a good hedge should be cropped
every year, but I'm glad I've seen the overgrown untidy ones

where the women gathered the blackberries in the autumn and we picked dewberries in late summer; where we sat with Walt and Tom out of the wind to eat our ten o'clock bait, tying the sweating horses on the 'burra' side of the hedge to some overgrown elm or ash, while Uncle George poured luke-warm tea out of his bottle into a folded copy of the day before's *Daily Chronicle* for 'Tiny', his liver and white spaniel, to lap up before it had time to get through the paper. Then there were the dry sticks and last year's leaves in the hedge bottom, good fuel for a dinner-time fire on a frosty winter's day. Hedges must be stock-proof to keep good neighbours, but an overgrown hedge is not an ugly thing.

CHAPTER THIRTY-THREE

TOMMY FLUTE OF BUMBO

UNCLE JIM worked for Tommy Flute as a young man. In fact they were both young then. They milked twelve cows and my uncle carried water to them in the winter, for Tommy kept them in the long shed and the water was in the pool behind the cider mill in the Home Orchard. Roan shorthorns, as much alike as peas in a pod, they were. When I knew Tommy he was fat, purple faced, rheumaticky and a widower who had buried two wives, and his family all grown up and gone. He kept a fair few pigs besides his cows and employed two men and an extra one for haymaking. He was a pretty hard drinker and his rheumatics just allowed him to get to the Plough and Harrow. One dark night he was making his way up the lane and somehow or other he lost his way and standing under a tall elm tree shouted, 'Man lost.' An owl in the tree answered 'Who, Who' and Tom shouted back, 'Tommy Flute of Bumbo.' The tree was by his yard gate and his housekeeper Rosie Sallis was waiting to help him up the stairs to his bedroom. As the years rolled by, Tommy became what is known as 'sweet' on Rosie, although he was a man well into his seventies.

Market days at Beckford, Tommy arrived home late, 'market hearted' from the inn, or as Tom Wheatcroft would say, 'About three parts drunk and the other part mad.' Rosie grew scared of these fortnightly market days and as she said to me, 'I've allus bin respectable.' In my youth in our old house we had no door keys except the front door one which we could lock from the outside. The general rule was bars from the inside of all the old doors. 'Have you put the bars up?' were often Dad's last words before he went to bed. These three-by-three-inch bars fitted nicely into a huge staple, square shape at one and the other end of the bar dropped into an 'L'-shaped fitting.

Rosie Sallis had a bar at her bedroom door on the inside. Tommy, coming home late from market, often found that Rosie had already gone to bed and put the bar up. One cold winter's night Tommy arrived and put his pony and trap away about eleven o'clock and Rosie had gone to bed. Tommy mounted the stairs and stood outside Rosie's barred bedroom door: 'Can I come in, Rosie, I be cold.' 'No, you *cannot*,' Rose replied from her room. Then the conversation went like this:

'Rosie!'

'Yes, Tommy?'

'When I was a little bwoy and I was cold, my mother used to cuddle I. Ud'st cuddle me tonight?'

Rosie was shocked at this and told him to go to his own room, whereupon Tommy took a crowbar and tried in his drink-fuddled way to break down Rosie's door, but these old elm doors don't respond easily to a crowbar and Tommy went cold to bed and Rosie gave her notice in next morning. Tommy wanting to be cuddled after market is still a legend up the lane.

Haymaking after the Big Seeds had been mown and the hay cocked and fit to carry found Tommy with his pony and trap driving alongside his horse and waggon, two pitchers and one loader loading the hay. Tommy wanted the hay 'up into one yup', as he said, 'afore it rains'. As the pitchers, one each side his waggon, reared the cocks of hay with their long shuppicks into the load and the waggon and horse moved to the next two cocks, Tommy was all impatient. You see, he had known the time when he was young and could have pitched a load with the best pitcher in the village.

'Hold tight, hold tight,' he kept shouting, almost before the pitchers had time to get their forkful on the waggon. This exclamation was an order for the well-experienced horse to move until the loader shouted, 'Whoa.'

'Don't thee hold tight too fast,' said Frank Wheatcroft, one of the pitchers he had borrowed off the Squire. This made no difference to Tommy who wanted 'the hay up together in one yup'. Frank bided his time; towards evening when the old maid (horse flies) had quietened down and the owl was hooting in Tommy's elm, Tommy nodded off to sleep in his pony trap. Frank crept up alongside, undid the leather traces which hooked the pony to the shafts and unbuckled the breeching straps and the pony stood there munching away at a heap of new-made hay. The haymakers finished, as Frank said, 'when it was dark under the hedges' and took their load to the rick. They clean forgot about old Tommy left snoring away in his trap and as the chill of the July night came on and the moon as big as a football came over Broadway Hill. Tommy woke with a start. There he was sitting in his trap in the middle of his hayfield. 'Gee up, Bonnie,' he said to the pony. The pony moved gently forward, slipping straight out of the shafts leaving Tommy high and dry in his trap. He climbed down, cursing the younger generation and left his trap behind and led his pony into the stable. Frank said, 'He never came nowhere anighst us agun till we had got the hay in, but mind you, Frederick'—Frank looked sad as he said it—'he cut our cider down to half a gallon a day after that.'

Frank went into the details of Tommy's funeral when he died at eighty-four. 'Never sin a mon uth such a belly when they screwed him down. I know cos I helped carry him, you could just see a part of his one hand peeping under the lid. Never sin a job like that afore. It was a hot day and he warmed our shirts a carrying him up the churchyard. If only he ad a knowed, he was having his own back, ya know.'

'Funny what you remember after the years go by. I always admired his roan shorthorns—they were a picture.'

CHAPTER THIRTY-FOUR

SPARROW AND PIGEON SHOOTS AND RABBIT COURSING

SOME MAY say that the exodus of so many town folk to our villages has led to a more humane approach to the birds and beasts of the field. This cannot be entirely denied. Our grandfathers, I am sure, never meant to be cruel to the wild life around them but at times were thoughtless, living to a pattern—a tradition—which had grown up with them.

The countryman has always thought of sport in terms of the chase. Whatever the end may have been, there is an inbred desire in his leisure time to be catching, hunting, shooting or snaring something. Often as not the end product, as we say today, was something to cook for his dinner. Without getting involved in any way with the rights and wrongs of fox hunting, let me make it plain from the start that I would like to see it continue, but there are certain things, almost rituals, which could be amended. On the other hand, so many people who know so little about the sport get so hot under the collar about it—a thing which a countryman like myself finds difficult, after seeing twenty or more laying hens lying dead on the fowlhouse floor, all with their heads bitten off by Reynard who had forced his way into the pen doing all this destruction and only eating a part of one bird. He's a rogue, but is still entitled to as humane a treatment as possible. His numbers must be controlled. If this could only be done without cub hunting in late summer when the pretty little creatures have not yet learnt the ways of escape of the wily old fox, I for one would be happier.

Different people have their own sense of values. It is difficult to have an unbiased opinion, but it does strike me that there seem to be more protests made, more hullaballoo against traditional country sports than there are against the insipid anaemic broiler fowl, produced like so many ball bearings in a factory, never seeing the light of day or the green fields. Then there is the battery hen cooped in a cage as an egg-laying machine. Oh yes, we do strain at a gnat and swallow a camel, and my view is that the scientist, the man at the drawing board who is responsible for these inventions for housing livestock in such intensive conditions, has caused infinitely more suffering than the men in hunting pink. Can you imagine the village blacksmith under his chestnut tree so much as ever thinking of manufacturing the hen battery, yokes to pen cattle for intensive baby beef production, sweat boxes for pigs to produce early bacon or pork—pigs which will catch pneumonia when they come in the fresh air if they are not slaughtered within hours? I feel that these things must be recorded before we are too critical, too intolerant of the way the ordinary working folk of our village and many others round the hill spent Boxing Day, one of the few holidays of the year away from the plough, the cattle, the hedging, the draining and all the things which country folk were wrapped up in earlier in the twentieth century.

For the sparrow and pigeon shoots, the rabbit coursing held in the Little Seeds behind the White Hart Inn, the organisers, led by the landlord, paid the village labourers a price per head for all the birds and rabbits they caught alive for the event; a penny a piece for the sparrow, more for the pigeons and rabbits. Just how the villagers caught them was described to me quite vividly by Frank Wheatcroft. Bird batting came second nature to the youths of our village. A bird bat is simply a net hung between two poles for catching birds. Nets could be bought in town but some of the village women knitted them for their own menfolk. They were made of tanned string—very similar to fishing nets. These were used on dark nights, and the method used to catch sparrows was quite simple. The youths took their net and poles and with one holding each pole and the nets held close to the hedge (not too taut), the other fellows beat the hedge on the other side with sticks. Then another of the party held a lantern at the back of the net and the sparrows flew for the light. The two chaps holding the poles closed in and trapped perhaps as many as six or seven birds at a time. This was best done the night before the shoot, then the birds were put into cages and kept until they were required.

I suppose bird batting has been a pastime for the younger villagers for centuries, sometimes to catch the birds for sparrow pies when times were hard and meat was just something to be talked about. Times when Grandfather spoke of having the smell of an oil rag with his bread for bait. Another likely place to catch sparrows was around the corn ricks in the rickyards. The sparrows which roosted under the thatch were easily caught, being attracted to the lantern as in beating the hedges. Of course sparrows were considered a great pest in the old days. The churchwardens paid out, quite regularly, pence per dozen for sparrow heads produced at their meetings.

The catching of the pigeons for these annual shoots presented very few problems. Dovecotes at the manor provided these. These old cotes housed what were known as duff pigeons—a type of rockdove. Frank Wheatcroft confided to me that catching them was 'uzzy money, a bob a piece mind tha shooters paid us'. Then he described the catching. 'Come dark,' he said, 'me and old Nailus Green went down to the Squires' with some of them wicker fowl crates; you sin um?' I agreed. 'Mind,' he said, 'thurs a hell of a lot of holes in a dovecote, but that one at the Squire's was uzzy, they never went back very dip. We stopped up all the holes at the top with old sack bags, got a plank that fitted the rows of holes at the bottom—the stone steps that we stood on be there now.' 'Yes,' I said, 'there are fantail pigeons there today.'

'Fantails and Tumblers was no good. We was arter Duff Pigeons. Now we was all set for the capture. Nailus held the lantern and we left one hole open to shine the light in, and as the birds came forward, I muzzled um and dropped um in the fowl crate. We only took what we wanted and left plenty to breed in the spring.'

'Where did Squire Humphrey come into this?' I asked.

'Oh, he never took no part in the sparrow and pigeon shoots, it was just a bit below him—mostly little men had a go at that.'

Oliver, that wily rabbit catcher, a legend of the hill, could be depended upon to provide plenty of live rabbits for the coursing. He caught them either with the long net at night or snared them with wires. 'But if you snare a rabbit, Frank,' I said, 'often as not it breaks its neck.'

'Ah,' Frank winked at me, 'shall I tell ya a secret? Put a knot in the wire so that the slip knot don't go tight and you have got him alive with a necklace on.' Then Frank described the actual happenings in the Little Seeds on those Boxing Days of long ago.

'Sam Dolphin who kept the White Hart was a sportsman, born and bred. A popular man who could shoot like a sniper. Now down at Sedgberrow where the land lies lower by the brook and works better than some of the cold clay of our parish, market gardening flourished,' Frank said, 'afore I was as big as a button. The Sedgberrow gardeners allus carried a gun, rabbits and gardening don't go together. You knows, Fred, avout me a telling ya that Bredon Hill have bin alive of rabbits afore the remembrance of man. We gev up the struggle against um on the hill years ago.' I had to agree that sometimes it was as if the whole earth was moving when rabbits came out at dusk on the top.

'The Sedgberrow men were the mainstay of the shooting and coursing. The little gardeners—the Winnets, the Stevens, the Hunts—were all crack shots. Then come the outscouts.'

'Outscouts?' I was a little puzzled. 'Outscouts' Frank described as labouring chaps who had a muzzle loader. They stood around the outside of the field ready to shoot any pigeon that got away. 'They didn't bother with the sparrows.'

'Now let's have the set-up, Frank—I've never seen it, you know, only remember what my father told me.' First of all Frank described it as a company of men, all in line by the Big Seeds gate and halfway up the field towards the wood were three traps. Take pigeon shooting for a start. Three pigeons were kept in the traps and a string was connected to the lid of each trap. Now none of the men with the guns knew what string was going to be pulled to open the trap and release the pigeon. They took it in turns with the firing and shot at the pigeons when they had flown clear of the trap. There was a kind of sweepstake and the one who shot the most birds won the money. Besides this, betting went on all day as the bookies gave out their odds, such as two to one on the bird, or two to one on the gun. A neighbouring keeper told me how he had been asked to take part in a pigeon shoot at the next village. He told me he could shoot along with the next but his pocket wasn't deep enough to keep up with the gambling, which often ended in a drunken fight at night. An observant man, he noticed how cruelly sometimes the man acted who put the pigeons out of the crate into the trap. 'Oh yes,' Mr. Archer,' said he, 'the men would break one wing so that the pigeon flew away slowly and easily,' adding the secret that the shooters had ordered this, then bet heavily on the gun as the pigeon would then be easy game—you can't miss a pigeon with a broken wing, he is almost like a sitting bird. Oh, the wisdom of age and experience. The gamekeeper who lives a solitary life thinks a lot, observes and is usually blessed with a hawk-like eye. My neighbour was such a man.

Bill Grimmit, an outscout from Hinton, had an old muzzle-loader and Frank recalled with a smile that as a youth watching the sport, if Bill let his gun off, you couldn't see Bill till the gun smoke went down. 'Talk about the H-bomb and the mushroom cloud,' he said, 'I a sin that seventy-five year ago.'

Sparrow shooting was much the same except that the guns used dust shot, a very small shot, to load their guns with. 'I a sin some capers uth guns,' Frank went on, 'and some close shaves, but never before nor since sin a mon fetch down sparrows like Sam Dolphin. If he thought someone was out of form or inexperienced he'd purposely let fly with his gun at the same time so that the other shooter thought he had at least killed one bird; devilish good sport was Sam.'

The coursing I almost forgot. Any villager, or someone from the neighbouring villages, who had a dog they fancied, took him to the Big Seed on Boxing Day. The rabbit was released in the middle of the field, given a start and then two dogs chased him, one against the other. This caused no end of amusement as to whether Joe Bradfield's Airedale would beat Stocky Hill's mongrel. 'No,' Frank said, 'they didn't need to be greyhounds or whippets to course rabbits at Ashton on Boxing Day.'

'Sam Dolphin brewed his own beer, and hellishly strong it was—a feow hops a floating about on top of your mug. No chemicals in it,' Frank said. 'Folks as gets drunk now be weak in the head. Why, the beer unt no different to cold tea, but I've seen um drink one pint theirself and see somebody drink another, then make out they be drunk.'

'Any other Boxing Day recollections from the White Hart?' I asked Frank.

'Oi, in the field wur the council houses be now, we played the navvys as built the railway line from Honeybourne to Cheltenham one year at football and gen um a licking. Then towards

tay time (course the pub was open all day) some of the Bradfields, Wheatcrofts and Hills ud start barefisted boxing. They
ud belt away at each other for an hour at a stretch prompted by
Sam's beer. Then they ud go and have another gutsful a beer
and come out and start again.'

'Funny way to spend Boxing Day,' I said.

'There was no ill feeling, mind—just seeing who was the best
man. Stocky Hill was useful with his fists and I remembers one
Boxing Day he made out he was drunk and Arthur Bradfield
thought I have never beat him yet, now's my chance. Off they
started, Stocky reeling about playing his part well, when Arthur
ketched him one on the nose. Then Stocky set about him and
gev him the master hiding he had ever had, knocking him ass
over yud one time after another. You midn't believe me, Fred,
but they was happy days. We made our own amusement; one of
the Hunts come over from Sedgberrow on a penny farthing
bike. We had our bread and cheese and a drop of cider. Then
there wus the girls, they have allus bin the same. We generally
took some of the Sedgberrow girls back down through the
Plough and Harrow yard and had a bit of a romp with um in
Land Close barn, then over the level crossing and to their cottages. We was just gallus bwoys then—nothing went on out of
place.'

'Any pigeon shoots now, Frank?' I said.

'Oi, clay pigeons, but it's mostly the young farmers as does
that, cartridges are expensive for one thing, but it's still good
sport to watch. Talking of shooting, when Squire Humphrey
busted up [ploughed] the Thurness with the steam tackle, I
helped Old Nailus to plough it back with the 'osses in the
spring. I was handy then with a catapult.' (Frank's fingers
moved as if he was catching hold of that forked stick again.)
'You can please yourself whether you b'lieve it or not, but I saw
Sally [a hare] sat on her form in a furrow and I killed her with
a pebble at a hundred yards. I practised every night and could
dout a candle with a lead shot which I made in a mould for my
forked stick at fifty yards. Some folks thinks that it's only the
gentry that have tasted pheasant meat but I used to get one for
Sunday dinner most weeks in a season. Oh yes, they was happy
days but things be different now.'

CHAPTER THIRTY-FIVE

COLTS ON THE SKYLINE

As LONG ago as I can remember, July has always been a month when animals, especially cattle and horses, are most likely to get out. By this I mean break through the fences and hedges and jump stone walls into the neighbouring field. In the case of cattle it happens when the bree fly worries them on sultry, thundery days which we get around apple christening day, or St. Swithin's, in the middle of the month.

One such muggy July evening, after the early mown sainfoin clover had been ricked on the hill, Mr. Carter from the back window of his dining room spotted colts on the skyline. 'Yes, master,' said Shepherd Marsh, 'they be up on the Captain's Hill, and thurs a shire entire [stallion] as stands over seventeen hands and ull set about them gelding colts of yours as sure as God made little apples.' Mr. Carter had just finished his tea and stood in the courtyard at the back of his dairy in his slippers, stripped to the shirt and the leg buttons of his tweed breeches undone. Bert Bradfield had been horse-raking with Bonnie, that chocolate-coloured old mare, down in the brook meadows. He was just bringing her in for tea and hanging her gear—cart saddle hames, collar and bridle—up in the saddle room.

'Bert,' Carter shouted, 'don't turn Bonnie out in the fields, we shall be wanting her, and come on in and have a mouthful of tea, I shall want you as well. Now, Fred, hurry and fetch your Dad, tell him it's urgent.'

From the rickyard at the back of Mr. Carter's vegetable garden, where the thatched bull-pen and cider mill stood, I could see nothing of the colts but I soon fetched Dad down from the top farm, calling for Tom Wheatcroft, the cowman, on the way. While these staid sons of the soil were debating and deciding which would be the best way to get the colts back into Spring Hill, I climbed up a ladder on to the top of the bull-pen to get a view of the skyline. There, between the stone wall of Spring Hill over on the Captain's Hill, stood a whole row of horses. They were just where the hill and the sky met.

'Bert, look sharp,' said Dad, 'and put Bonnie's mullen [bridle] on. The shepherd says she will 'tice the colts back through the bridle gate.' Bert didn't need telling that he could ride up the eight-hundred-foot hill while we all walked with sticks, Mr. Carter and the shepherd carrying in turn a little bag with some of the shepherd's ewe and lamb food in it. This was also to 'tice the colts. I delved my hand in the bag and fetched out a few locust beans and chewed them as we ascended the hill.

'We're gwain to have some pantomime uth that entire,' warned Tom Wheatcroft. 'He's along with about half a dozen mares and he'll knock the daylights out of them two-year-old geldings.'

When we think of colts, often known as knobby colts, we imagine animals with long, ungainly legs, small bodies and just playful. I had another think coming when we drew near to the two-year-olds—seven of them which Dad and Mr. Carter had bought as yearlings at Gloucester Barton fair. They looked massive to me, a little boy in jersey and knickers, wearing my first pair of hobnailed boots and carrying a nut stick to give a little confidence—and goodness me I needed it.

Bert opened the bridle gate and stood just inside the Captain's Hill with Bonnie. The stallion whinnied and Bonnie answered back. The Captain's stallion then charged towards us open-mouthed. Bert, a cool and fearless fourteen-year-old, held Bonnie quite still and I trembled as I mounted the Cotswold stone wall and felt safer. Meanwhile Mr. Carter, Dad, the shepherd and Tom Wheatcroft were rounding up the colts and persuading them to go and join Bonnie. They backed and kicked and reared and Tom Wheatcroft and the shepherd agreed that what they wanted was about a fortnight's work on a piece of fallow to knock some of the devil out of them, and then turning up again.

'I'd just like four of them customers hooked on to a Lark-worthy scuffle a rooting them clats of clay over on the fallow in Thurness,' Tom Wheatcroft told the company. 'We had used to hook um on to a darn great elm tree years ago,' the shepherd added, 'and udn't they sweat. They be green, ya see, and soon goes all of a lather. But what's the good of me talking, I shall blooming soon be seventy.'

Mr. Carter tried 'ticing with the sheep food, Bonnie ate some but the colts weren't hungry and galloped once more around the Captain's Hill.

'Ockud place to get um back from,' Tom observed. 'I remembers the time they held hoss races in this field, he's forty acres if he's a chain.'

Dad told Bert to take Bonnie to a hollow piece of ground just below a belt of fir trees. I reluctantly followed them, trying my hardest not to appear afraid, but I had heard gruesome stories as I sat on the corn bin in the stable with Walt, about stallions that would bite through the back of your neck and crush you against stone walls. But it was not the Captain's stallion I should have been afraid of. It happened like this. Bonnie, Bert and I were standing in the hollow waiting for yet another round up of the colts and sure enough towards us they came like the front row in the Grand National. I suppose my height at the time was summed up by Tom as about 'four foot and a tater'. As the seven fit, sleek geldings came towards Bonnie, they slowed up all but one on the left flank just where I stood. He saw me, but it was too late for him to swerve or stop and he jumped clean over the top of me and as I write so many years after, the picture of his hooves passing over the top of my head remains so vivid in my mind. He joined the other six; at last they saw sense and followed Bonnie and Bert through the bridle gate back into Spring Hill.

They were all fetched off the hill for the autumn ploughing on the sticky clay of the vale. Walt, Tom and Bert took some of the nonsense out of them as they worked them two at a time in the four-horse teams. What a grand lot they turned out to be. Short and Sharper, two chestnuts were sold to a neighbouring market gardener the following spring and Jim Bradfield ploughed the two-horse land with them and told Dad one day, 'It's the certin truth, gaffer, they be as hardy a pair of 'osses as ever I worked with, they be sensible as Christians—no vice, no nastiness about them.'

Little Blackbird was my favourite. He was what is known as a 'durgin'—a carthorse in miniature. He stood less than fifteen

hands, was black apart from a white face like a badger, white
feet and a soft mouth and silky pink nose. He had one draw-
back, he was blind in one eye. Neither Dad nor Mr. Carter ever
knew how it happened and I didn't let on when I heard of a boy
with a catapult one Sunday afternoon causing poor little Blackbird to lose his one eye. There was no room for Blackbird in the
stable, so he occupied a loose-box on the left of the door. Tom
Wheatcroft and myself made a special point of feeding him
with the best food we could lay our hands on. We gave him
linseed cake, stolen from the shepherd's granary, oats we robbed
the milking cows of, but it was worth it all to see his coat shine
like velvet and he was always so willing, yet awkward to drive in
a dray owing to his one eye. Yes, Blackbird did everything but
talk. I talked to him and I'm certain he understood.

CHAPTER THIRTY-SIX

THE COUNTRYMAN AT HOME

It is difficult to imagine as we live here in houses and cottages of all types and ages, what life is like in some great city. True, so many of our villagers now work in the smaller towns around and 'commute'—that awful word which means travelling morning and night to their careers.

The village life of my boyhood was simplicity itself. The men all left home at six forty-five, the stockman earlier, often carrying with them their lunch in a straw frail basket and the day-men their spades, bill hooks, shuppicks, hoes and the simple tackle they required for the day's work. At half past five in the evening one saw the homeward trudge. The frail, now devoid of food and drink but filled with wood chips and spails from the fallen tree, or occasionally a rabbit for late dinner the next day. In summer-time after tea, everybody was busy in the vegetable garden among the potatoes, the beans and the cabbages. The more ambitious grew onions of enormous size for the local shows and the pig in the garden sty ate all that the family left over. I think one of the striking changes in village life has been the use that the cottage garden has been put to. In the past potatoes were vital; so were the runner beans, onions and so forth. Today the flowers hold pride of place. In our village a few forget-me-nots, roses, columbines and sweet peas were the sum total of the cottage garden flowers. Oh, I did forget phlox and night-scented stocks—but today every flower and variety of flower in the catalogues can be seen in our gardens and the villagers are saying it's cheaper to buy potatoes in the town than grow them. Allotments are almost as dead as the dodo. In fact in some circles it is a dirty word.

It's good to think though that after a full day in factory and office our new countryman can please himself and grow flowers for pleasure and just a little salad stuff, and potter in the greenhouse among his tomatoes.

The harvest of the garden crop has ceased to be as extremely important as it used to be when our villagers relied so much on home-grown vegetables. But to live in a village after years of city life must be an eye-opener for anyone. Being a native you just believe about half what you hear and take the rest with a pinch of salt. The tales that get around are fantastic; they often get back to one and it's common knowledge what time Mr. So and So gets up in the morning, how often he cleans his car, when he has a new suit—and however do they manage to dress the children on his wages? and his wife's last dress from Cheltenham must have cost the earth! 'The car's the firm's, so they say, oh, and did you hear about the cheque that bounced at the grocers?'

I suppose the answer to all this is to grow an extra thick skin, but it is annoying sometimes when often somebody will start wicked lies, especially about newcomers who haven't yet been accustomed to the ways of the village, and have not yet grown that extra skin.

Let no one say what a pity the old life has gone, but let us all say with the old folk 'things be different than years ago'. In many ways life is better. So many of us look back with a touch of sadness when we think of the ploughman 'Homeward plodding his weary way'. I have to say, quoting an old ploughman that 'if they brings back the 'osses, whose a gwain to gu along with um?'

It is pictures such as these that are so easy to recollect if only we think back just a few years. Tom Wheatcroft always told me that the best pictures a working man could have hung up in his kitchen were flitches of bacon. 'I beun't much of a judge of art,' he said, 'although I minds the time when I have sat along with Tiddley, that artist who had his studio in the old cheese room atop a thee fayther's cart shed. Mind tha, he could do a landscape, you a got one of his best in your house—bottom of the stairs.' I agreed it was very realistic. 'Realistic, be hanged for a tale, it's a picture of the moat, two yows and four lambs under that hawthorn anant the stile into the sheep barn orchard. Dust thee know, Fred, when he painted that un with the hawthorn in full blow I fancied I could smell the blossom. The ship [sheep] they was Cotswolds—haven't seen none for years. They be too big for present-day housewives, but I remember seeing legs of

Cotswold mutton carved at the harvest suppers. Mind, we didn't say no to a bit of fat then a day. Thurs ony two legs on a ship though.' I felt Tom with his thoughts, never daring to ask him his views on modern art. Other pictures come to mind—the rain-water butt, usually an old hogshead barrel turned sour. Then there was the pig swill barrel where such a variety of things went in.

'Pigs be particular,' Blenham once told me. 'Their stomach and our be amus the same. Dust thee remember old Dr. Overthrow?' I said I did, just before he finished. 'Well,' Blenham continued as he half stood and half leant against our courtyard wall, 'he did operations just arter that one on King Edud. Skilful man with the knife was our doctor and I'm a gwain to tell tha summat now as thee mindust not swallow.'

'Go on, Blenham, I'll buy it,' I said.

'Boy, it's as true as this ash plant's in my hand. Dr. Overthrow operated on pigs at the bacon factory in A'sum, just to get his hand in afore he started on humans; now whether a pig a got an appendix or no I can't tell ya.'

'If pigs are like humans,' I asked Blenham, 'what about the swill?'

'The swill,' he said, 'is the leftovers from the cottagers' meals —bread, taters, the scrapings from the plates, sour milk and the like. This, mixed with barley meal and some more taters boiled in their skins and made all of a monnsey [a pomace] in the missus' dolly tub—a bit of spice and it wouldn't hurt you nor me.'

'What about germs and viruses?' I said.

'Lors, bless the fellow, when thee bist my age, thee ut be immune to them.'

Around the farms in our village, in the rickyards, the cowsheds and granaries, the hens scratched around the cockerels and the long-spurred cocks strutted as if they had the right to enter every building, the right to sample any foodstuffs around. Yes, the barndoor hens had enjoyed this position for so many generations. They scratched the muck buries for worms, they obtained their grit from the village street, and on a bare patch in our rickyard where the grass has been killed by the scratching over the years of our hundred or so fowl, we fed them twice a day, broadcasting the mixture—half wheat and half kibbled maize—calling the stragglers from their hiding places—bid, bid, bid, bid and whistling, as near as I remember, fee-oo, fee-oo, fee-oo. In winter-time Dad cooked potatoes and fed them hot mashed with Sussex grown oats and a little spice. This was their morning breakfast. Where did the fowl roost at night? Come with me on a winter's night with a lantern around the buildings. In our old stone barn with the blue lias threshing floor, the beams ran across the width of the roof and across those beams the fruit picking ladders were stored away for the winter. In fact, all the ladders were there except the strong thirty-rung one with the iron spiked feet which Tom Wheatcroft used to start a cut on the hay ricks. First of all the hens fled up into the tallet and from there it was a mere flutter for them to reach the ladders. The more agile Anconas—a breed which so easily becomes airborne—reached to the height of the barn while the stately Light Sussex cocks perched on the railings surrounding the calf-pens. The sight on the hay loader which stood just inside the barn with its rows and rows of lathes horizontal and joined together with cords, looked as if it had been designed for one purpose—a hen roost on wheels.

As we stood there on a winter's night, the calves licking our hands and pulling at our coats (they were just curious about the lantern), it made one think of a portion of the terrace at Villa Park just at the beginning of an International match. The hens looked as if they had been placed, row by row, in such precision. They craned their necks at the lantern and a few more droppings fell between the rows of sleepers adding to the heap of the real stuff which accumulated at the foot of the loader all the winter.

As we entered the empty stable, the odd rat bolted down his hole from the wooden mangers where he had been cleaning up a few odd bits of bait left by the horses when they were turned out on to the fields soon after tea. The odd early broody hen ruffled her feathers and squawked disapprovingly as we shone the light on her as she was sitting tight on a few eggs. While we think of eggs, egg collecting was an exciting business. No, the eggs didn't roll down out of wire cages in an orderly fashion; these eggs had to be won. Sometimes we lay on our sides and reached them from an awkward spot under an old manger. This was fairly simple providing a broody hadn't decided to be sitting there.

It was dark under these mangers and I have put my hand on a hedgehog, but never mind, I was paid a penny a dozen for all eggs which I found which were not laid in the usual places; for instance, the rows of pot hampers lined with hay in the dark corners under the tallet.

Some laid in the many clumps of stinging nettles in the springtime—no one had thought of using sodium chlorate to destroy the nettles in those days just after the First World War. But what a pleasant surprise when a hen hatched her brood of chicks in such places. Dad and I would move the brood after dark, away from the harm of rats, and there was always a possibility of a fox coming down off the hill and taking them. An old tea chest and a bit of wire and soon the mother hen was safe with her chicks and as we said 'she had stolen her nest'—what a picture!

CONCLUSION

As I HAVE written about our people and their ways, lots of thoughts have come to mind. These are not a wishful thinking that the past with its interest, its individuality, could be recaptured on some large scale just for the sake of it, and that progress and efficiency should go by the board—no, that could never be and it is just as well.

I have in mind something much less ambitious—something quite small compared with the vastness of projects in these days. Societies which I am associated with are struggling against costs to re-create folk villages—villages as they were in the nineteenth century and before with the folk industries. This is all good both for our young people and for tourists from abroad.

Don't you sometimes wonder as I do how exciting it would be for this country of ours (before it's too late) to have one or more farms run on nineteenth-century lines?

We spend millions on space research, trying to reach the moon, but for quite a modest sum, farms could be set aside as show places—not places where a robot tractor ploughs unmanned, but places where our children could visit from the schools, or visitors from abroad. I don't mean agricultural museums where a plough stands—these have their place, but what I was really thinking of was a number of acres of land, ploughed with simple tackle—the four-horse team tandem of four Shire horses, a pair of Suffolks abreast harrowing and drilling the ground, the horse mower and the horse binder in use. There are, I believe, some sets of steam engines left to show us how steam cultivating was done; the steam engine and threshing machine. There is no need for me to elaborate and explain the possibilities, but if this scheme were run properly by the state it would attract hordes of people to see the usual round of events of ploughing, cultivating, planting, mowing, reaping, threshing—all done by horses with horse implements and the simple tackle.

This enterprise could also include chicks hatched as I mentioned in the previous chapter, ricks built and thatched. So many of our fifty-one million people today have never had the chance to see, work with and enjoy the work on the land done by the simple tackle.

As I sit here by my own late autumn fireside, I can visualise large car parks having to be provided to cope with the onlookers. No, this isn't just pie in the sky, sincerely it is a call from my heart. I hope we never lose sight of our past agricultural history. Someone once said that if any man could make two blades of grass grow where one grew before, he would be one of the greatest benefactors to mankind. Agricultural science has almost achieved this and yet millions starve in the world today. My suggestion, I am afraid, won't solve that problem, but at least it is something to feed the minds of an intensively bred, battery-housed people.